A
Call Girl's
Best Sex
Tips

THIS IS A CARLTON BOOK

Text and design © Carlton Books Ltd 2009

This edition published in 2009 by Carlton Books Limited
20 Mortimer Street
London W1T 3JW

10 9 8 7 6 5 4 3 2 1

Material in this book has previously appeared in *Foreplay & Fellatio*
(2007), *How to Be a Sex Goddess* (2004), *Satisfaction Guaranteed:
350 Best Sex Tips Ever* (2003), *Sex in the City* (2003), *Sex in the City:
Day & Night* (2005), *Over 100 S&M Sex Tips* (2008) and *Over 100
Daring & Deviant Fetish Sex Tips* (2008).

A CIP catalogue record is for this book is available from the
British Library.

ISBN 978 1 84732 557 0

Printed in China

A Call Girl's Best Sex Tips

500 how-tos and dos
to turn him on

Renée Dubois

CARLTON
BOOKS

Contents

Introduction

**According to statistics, one in ten men use professional sex
providers – for as many different reasons as there are men,
but the thrill factor is definitely high on the list. It's not just
sex with a stranger that has allure, but the feeling of illicit
transgression, and of having the woman make all the moves.
The tables are turned: she listens to him, seduces him and
initiates the sex. A call girl is also trained to know the needs
of men and to fulfil fantasies, especially ones that many men
feel their girlfriends or wives will not.**

According to psychologists, the appeal lies in the fact that the
call girl is fully devoted to the man without expecting anything
(other than money) in return. She's devoted to his pleasure, and
he doesn't need to make her happy or worry about her emotions.
Even though this is all an illusion, it taps into the man's need to
be cared for and not to be judged. On the following pages you
will find tips and advice to help create that experience and
excitement at home with your partner – from seduction ideas
to a varied and extensive range of tricks and games.

In th sex industry subculture, certain code words have emerged
to communicate the description of explicit acts. For example,
"incall" means that the session takes place at the call girl's
location whereas "outcall" means that the session is selected by
the customer. A range of different acts or services are usually
described by abbreviations (see pages 248–53). For example, you
might offer your lover the Girlfriend Experience – known in sex

ads as GFE and which offers the idea, however false, that you are actually on a date. You talk, confide, provide companionship and affection, and actually kiss, which is where many prostitutes draw the line. Sometimes there's no penetrative sex, although it's permitted. Or you could offer a PSE – Porn-star Experience – which entails everything you can imagine, all done without a condom. Other treats could include a Snow Blow (fellatio with ice cubes) or a Fire and Ice (a blowjob swapping hot tea with ice). These, and more, can be incorporated into your lovemaking and role-play or used in dirty talking or cybersex.

All in all, providing a call girl service at home for your partner is easy and safe – and there's no gritty reality (STDs, being "found out", and the girl isn't doing it to make rent or pay for drugs). With all the downsides associated with the actual thing, a bit of role-playing with a consensual partner seems the perfect option. On the following pages you will find professional erotic tips to mimic the thrill and excitement of a call girl scenario. The ideas offered cover the full spectrum of sexual experience, from seduction and foreplay through sex positions and sex acts to fantasy and fetish – everything to give your guy a good time, whoever you might be that night! Learn to role-play and seduce, how to dress to make him hot, and get the inside track on all the little mouth moves and kissing tips that make him moan. From novel sex positions to tantalizing touches and rubs, you'll master all the tricks porn-stars and pros use, and more!

Chapter 1
Work Your Assets

FIND YOUR INNER SEX GODDESS

As Sophia Loren said, "Sex appeal is 50 per cent what you've got and 50 per cent what people think you've got", so get in touch with your inner sex goddess to maximize your female allure. The most ordinary-looking women are capable of charming and disarming the most gorgeous men simply because they have attitude. A true sex goddess has confidence in herself. When a man compliments her on her body, she does not reply, "Oh my God, no! You must be joking! I'm huge!" She doesn't give men the chance to judge her and find her wanting by investing their opinions with too much power.

If a man is rude or thoughtless, or insensitive, a sex goddess knows to walk away. She doesn't stick around hoping she'll be the one to change him. She knows exactly what she wants, and more importantly, she understands precisely what she needs from a sexual encounter or a relationship. And if she's unlikely to be satisfied, she doesn't pursue it. In short, she knows she's gorgeous and that she deserves the best. This is not arrogance, it's pure self-belief. Basically, no one treats her badly – they wouldn't dare!

GIVE YOURSELF A MAKEOVER
Knock-'em-out beauty is within your control.

1 Get a facial. Studies have revealed that the one thing that's guaranteed to make his head do a 360-degree turn is smooth, shiny skin (glossy hair doesn't hurt either). It's a sign of high oestrogen levels and mimics the signs of youthfulness and fertility.

2 Dye your hair blonde. Research has found that blondes are more likely to be seen as eye candy than people with darker coloured hair.

3 Get dolled up. When a New Mexico State University study recorded beauty preferences, it was found that the look that made his eyes pop is a high forehead, full lips, a short jaw, a small chin and nose, big eyes and knife-sharp cheekbones. In short, Barbie lives.

4 Do your abs. A university of Texas study suggests that men prefer a 0.7 waist-to-hip ratio (ie, when the hips are roughly a third larger than the waist), possibly because it broadcasts a female's health and readiness to breed. For the record, Cindy Crawford and Naomi Campbell inch in with a 0.69 ratio, but so does anyone with a 70 cm (28 in) waist and 100 cm (40 in) hips – which just so happens to be 47 per cent of the UK female population.

DOUBLE TAKES

Consider yourself warned: these subtle but totally sexifying beauty moves will inexplicably draw every man in the area directly towards you.

1 Spellbind him with lips he'll lust for. – a berry shade whispers seductively, while a deep vibrant red shouts "Look at Me".

2 Tempt him to touch you by massaging baby oil into your skin. Go out and enjoy your new high TQ (touchability quotient) by "accidentally" brushing your bare arm against a cute guy's biceps. Instead of apologizing, simply smile – silky, seductive skin means never having to say you're sorry.

3 Captivate him with cleavage. While a push-up bra can make your bosom perk up, a subtle golden shimmer will make it stand out among the masses. For a stare-if-you-dare divide, smooth on a sparkling, sheer liquid bronzer from collarbone to cleavage, concentrating some colour in between your breasts to create the illusion of a deep, lusty neckline.

4 Eroticize your scent. If you want your scent to draw in guys like bees to honey, avoid the number one fragrance faux pas: perfume overload. Forgo heavy scents for a subtle citrus fragrance that he'll sneak up closer to sniff.

CREATE CHEMISTRY

You can't score if you're not playing the field. Ninety per cent of life is about showing up in the first place. Go out to places with signs of life – intelligent or otherwise – and use these tricks.

1 Dress like you're a success. When researchers showed photographs of one particular woman to a group of men, either dressed comfortably or professionally, the men rated the nicely dressed version to be much more appealing, without realizing it was the same woman.

2 Make the first move. Ninety per cent of men polled said they would love to be approached by a woman.

3 Be seen in the right places. A New England centre for the Study of the Family discovered that where you meet someone for the first time can strongly influence attraction. For instance, when men met a woman in the gym, they thought she was sexy and healthy-looking, but when they ran into the same woman in the pub, they rated her as unattractive.

4 Get in his line of vision so that he notices you. Ninety-nine per cent of attracting a guy's attention is about getting him to see you in the first place.

5 If you go out with a group of friends or even just one girlfriend, make sure you separate off from them so that you appear to be more approachable. No man wants to be rejected in front of a group of women and he may well feel he can't approach you when you are protected by a herd of gatekeepers.

HEAD MOVES TO MAKE HIM NOTICE YOU
Sometimes all he needs is a nod in the right direction.

1 Toss your head. This is the classic attention-grabbing move
Flip your head back so that your face tilts upwards. The
movement attracts his eye as your face catches the light.
It means, "Hi, look at me."

2 Let him know you care with a flip of the hair. Raise one hand
and push your fingers through your hair. This can be done
once, slowly and thoughtfully, or in short spurts, pulling your
hair back and drawing attention to your face. He'll think
you're gorgeous and come your way.

3 The head nod is usually done when you're passing almost
nose to nose. Nod your head gently backwards and forwards
until you're communicating by moving together in a gentle
sway. It's a quick way to tell him, "Come with me, I'm more
than interested."

4 The eyebrow flash is the first of what psychologists call
"The Looks". Raise both eyebrows in an exaggerated gesture,
follow by lowering your eyes quickly to establish eye contact
momentarily. As the eyebrows rise to their peak, the eyeballs
are exposed because the eyelids lift and the muscles around
the eyes stretch, allowing more light on to the surface of the
eyes. This makes them appear large and bright and very
attractive. It's a genetically programmed classic come-on.

5 Tilt your head to one side and smile. You trigger a subtle sexual arousal in him by revealing a portion of your neck – even though the gesture suggests a certain demureness. The more you tilt your head, the more you're showing your interest. Throw lip–licking and side-glancing into the mix and you'll have him on his knees.

WORK YOUR BODY
These body moves are sure to entice him.

1 Crossing your arms is a natural, instinctive response when you're feeling vulnerable. The problem is it signals Do Not Approach! To avoid doing this, put one hand in your pocket, on your hip, or on the arm of a chair. Or hold something like a drink or a pen (useful for exchanging phone numbers).

2 Working out is a great way to get male attention – not because you might meet guys at the gym (although you probably will) but because you will love the way a strong healthy body feels when you have the energy and ability to do anything. When you're comfortable with yourself, you inevitably come across as being more confident, sexy and fun.

3 Practice a sexy walk. Stand up straight, take a stride about one and a half times the length of your foot. This is the distance men are biologically fine-tuned to read as a sign of health and fertility, making you a hot prospect for passing on their genes.

4 When you slide onto a bar stool, sit with your legs crossed at the knee in what's called the Leg Twine. To wrap him around your little toe, languidly stroke your calf and let your shoe fall partly off.

5 Get the same effect from a distance by crossing your legs so they point towards a nearby cutie, showing that you'd like to enter his personal space (about 1 m/ 3 ft, according to studies).

6 When you greet him, give off a sensual and warm aura when you're standing simply by resting your weight on one foot more than the other. Let your hip jut out a bit with your hands on the small of your back.

7 As you talk with him, point your knees, feet, hands, shoulders or whole body towards him – it's a subtle way of saying that you aren't complete strangers any more.

8 Affectionate touching tells a guy that you like him and that you wouldn't mind touching him more in private. If he says something witty, squeeze his forearm gently and laugh. If you want to go to the ladies' room, put your hand on his shoulder and say, "I'll be right back."

9 Copy him – when two people become captivated with each other, they begin to subtly and unconsciously mimic each other's postures and gestures within five to fifty seconds. Eventually, even breathing and heartbeats become synchronized. Called "mirroring", it's a learned habit left over from infancy when the newborn's body movements mimic the rhythmic patterns of whatever voice is speaking. You can consciously use mirroring to lure him in by deliberately echoing his movements. But keep it down to less than five gestures or he's going to feel stalked.

NO-TOUCH SEDUCTION TIPS

Here's a few ideas on how to get a man to approach you without lifting even a finger.

1 Get a flushed face by thinking of something sexy or embarrassing. It's a signal to him that you're attracted.

2 Guys are suckers for long hair. So entwine him in your locks by running your fingers through your hair and tossing it in his direction.

3 Scrub your tongue with a toothbrush every time you clean your teeth. Let it slide out a little when your target is near. A healthy pink tongue is a visual turn-on for him.

4 When we first notice someone we spend about three seconds scanning their face, flicking our eyes backwards and forwards between the other person's eyes. We then move down to the mouth and finish off with a few broader sweeps that take in the hair. Extending the scan to four and a half seconds will create strong emotions in him.

5 Buy time with a smile. Studies have found that when you smile at someone they take a longer look because they are made to feel at ease.

6 Your eyes are 18 times more sensitive than your ears. Use them to captivate him. Holding his gaze for two seconds is the magic number – any shorter than this and he can't be sure you're interested; any longer and he might call the cops.

7 Try the two-eyed wink. A slower version of a normal blink, with all the playfulness (and none of the cheese factor) of a regular wink. Glance his way, then blink slowly and smile. Wait for him to smile in response, then look away again.

8 Go for the kill by sidling up next to him and letting him feel your heat. Stand so close that you're almost touching him. When you step into his personal space, he interprets it as an immediate sexual invitation. If you stand close enough to a man for him to kiss you, he'll probably try.

9 Lick your lips when you look at him. Wet lips seem to simulate vaginal lubrication, signalling that he makes you horny.

10 Stroking your lower neck can cause your nipples to become firm. He'll happily take things from there.

WHAT TO WEAR TO BED

It's easier to start with what not to wear. Avoid anything featuring cartoon characters, cute slogans like "Cuddle Me" or "I Need a Hug" or anything made of brushed cotton. Unless he has a granny fetish, it's unlikely he'll be tempted to find out what's underneath your floral-sprigged tent-sized nightie. Boudoir-wear is an art. It's not acceptable to throw on a ripped oversized old T-shirt every night, comfortable though it is – it's not a look that screams "Take me".

Despite the variety of gorgeous lingerie shops, some men are still really bad at buying sex-wear for women. Crotchless scarlet lace rarely enhances anybody's best bits, unless their labia happens to be particularly stunning. If he's buying, head him in the direction of one of the many lingerie emporiums offering edgy, sexy but well-made items. Rather than nylon nasties you'll be getting something that will feel great against your skin and put you in the mood. Convince him that this is something that will benefit him.

Although sex-wear is not the same as sleepwear, the two can be combined in the form of, say, a see-through baby doll. However, do keep a selection of boudoir-wear set aside for special romantic occasions; there will be no doubt as to what's on the agenda if he sees you in these. Your sex-wear should consist of at least one outfit (or single item) that enhances all your assets and makes you feel devastatingly sexy.

When buying underwear, don't worry about whether the items will show under clothes. Instead ask yourself, "Do I look a million dollars in this?" Look for lace, silk, satin, ribbons, mesh and bows. Cleavage-enhancing corsetry or tight-fitting but silky gowns will show off your figure. Most men are wildly excited by red or purple underwear, so consider deviating from basic black. Obviously, avoid stretch nylon, sporty cotton and anything serviceable that looks as though you could carry shopping home in it. Pretty G-strings are great, small panties fine but big butt-grippers are not. The best ones are those that tie at the sides – sometimes known as "stripper knickers".

HOISERY
Ah yes, hosiery... There are some men who actually prefer tights (pantyhose), but they tend to have grown up in the 1970s when "American Tan" was not yet a term of abuse. On the whole, you're safer with stockings. Go for black or fishnet. Unless you are very thin or getting married, avoid white hosiery – it will make your legs look like undercooked sausages.

Try lacy hold-ups or stockings. They look great, provide easy access to underwear (which always goes on top of suspenders/garters and never underneath) and tap directly into every man's sexual fantasy list. Generally, suspenders (garters) are sexier than hold-ups because they are more traditional and they don't leave strange pink elastic-marks around your thighs. If they're just too fiddly to put on, leave the hold-ups on throughout sex and he'll be so excited he'll never know the difference.

ACCESSORIES AND FOOTWEAR

Naturally, most women wouldn't wear shoes to bed. But even if you're a sporty sneaker girl who walks like a newborn giraffe in heels, a pair of boudoir shoes is a good investment. "Fuck me shoes" as they are technically known feature stiletto heels, ankle straps or ribbons and pointy toes. They have the effect of elongating your legs and enhancing the curve of your butt – and also put your man in mind of a little light bondage. Obviously, feminism is not making its presence overtly clear here, but you can always lecture him on equal rights later, once you've tied him to the bedpost.

Of course the old call-girl standby of thigh-high boots is also a winner in the bedroom – but only if you've got legs like Julia Roberts in *Pretty Woman*, otherwise you run the risk of looking like Puss in Boots. Much safer are marabou fluffy mules with a 10-cm (4-in) heel, as worn by Marilyn Monroe and a variety of 1950s glamour models. Supplement your boudoir range with a selection of negligees, silk wraps, peignoirs and kimonos to float around the house. Add chiffon shawls, long strings of pearls and even chain belts and nipple rings or piercings – try fake ones if you don't fancy suffering unnecessary pain just to draw attention to your erogenous zones.

DRESSING TO UNDRESS

It's not just what you wear, but how you take it off. Opt for an outfit that accentuates your assets. For example, if your breasts are best, wear a cleavage-catapulting bustier. For bottom babes, go for a bum-revealing G-string.

Try switch-hitting by stripping him. Slowly undo his shirt. Gently slide if off, kissing and licking his chest. Get down on your knees and remove his shoes and socks. Fondle his penis through his pants as you slip them off. He'll be putty in your hands.

STRIPTEASE DOS

- Do slip down one bra strap before the other, very slowly, before undoing your bra.

- Do dangle the bra in front of him before dropping it on his lap.

- Do choose a front-closing bra to avoid any passion-killing fumbling and fiddling.

- Do keep your heels on till the last minute. They'll lengthen your legs and make 'em look like something that's just strolled out of a porn flick.

- Do wear stockings or lace hold-ups. You can give him a triple-X view by sitting on a chair and lifting one leg at a time, then rolling the stocking s-l-o-w-l-y down with your palms. He'll be howling oo-la-la.

STRIPTEASE DON'TS

- Don't wear anything with tricky sleeve cuffs –
  or undo them first so that you don't have to stop
  when slipping your shirt off.

- Don't choose tight-necked tops – you don't want
  to get stuck mid-strip looking more like a turtle
  than eye candy.

- Don't wear clothes with elasticated waistbands;
  they leave very unsexy marks on the skin.

Top Ten Tips To Successful Stripping

1 Place your hands on the fastening of your top and stroke your fingers over the zipper or buttons to give the impression that you might just possibly be thinking about undoing them.

2 Maintaining seductive eye contact, slide the zip down or undo the buttons, and then turn away from him and remove your top. Keeping your hands over your breasts, turn back to face him.

3 Slide your hands down over your hips to your skirt fastening. Again, play with the zip – slide it down a little one way then back up again to tease him.

4 Undo your skirt or trousers and turn away again. Now bend forward a little (straight legs, naturally) and allow your clothes to fall to the floor. If it's a small garment, kick it aside or use the toe of your shoe to toss it upwards, catch it and fling it to him.

5 With your hands over your breasts, face him again and dance slowly, gliding your hands up and down your body. Slide a bra strap down and then back up to tease him. Let both straps drop but keep your bra in place with your hands. Reach down to the back and unclip it, but don't let it drop yet…

6 Now turn away again so he can admire your butt. Let your bra fall, and then reach down gracefully and throw it to him while still facing away from him. Place your hands over your breasts and turn back to face him. To reveal your breasts, slowly slide your hands down to the sides of your panties.

7 Tease him a bit more. Pull the sides of your panties down a little way, or pretend to undo the ribbons. Pull the front down as far as it will go without revealing any pubic hair. Turn around again and slip your panties down then step out of them neatly. Kick them aside or to him.

8 Nearly there. Except for shoes and stockings you are now naked and it's perfectly acceptable to stop at this point if you want. But if you prefer full nudity, take off your shoes. Standing on one leg, undo each clip and slowly roll each stocking down (if you're less flexible, place one foot at a time on the bed or rest your foot on the chair he's sitting on), then pull it off with a flick of the wrist. Reach down to unclip your suspender (garter) belt and whip it away.

9 Continue to dance in front of him just out of reach until he can't bear it another second. You may then cross the room and begin to undress him.

10 If you're shy, and most of us are when it comes to taking off our clothes in a lit room, conceal as you reveal with a strategically placed feather boa. You can also add glamorous old-school accessories such as elbow-length gloves, a string of beads or a silk scarf. Use them to add to your performance, covering yourself with the boa or scarf as you slowly remove your lingerie.

DRESSING (TO SEDUCE) FOR THE WEEKEND

FRIDAY
Start the day in red – teddy, camisole, panties and/or bra. Then slip on a silk or velvet shirt that comes off with a quick flick of the wrist (Velcro-tabbed or via snaps or ties). After-hours pull out the stops – with all-out cleavage and a long strand of beads dangling in between. Later, just wear the baubles. As things heat up, use them to tease and please your lucky lad, running them across his skin and wrapping them around his limbs. Then roll them into a ball and knead his body into a state of bliss.

SATURDAY
Get your booty shaking by giving him a lap dance. Do like the professionals. Keep your guy fully clothed and make sure you're only wearing a G-string and heels. Absolutely forbid him to touch you (although you can touch him) – it'll give you a sexy, powerful feeling, and seeing your naked body but not being able to touch it will make him crazed with desire. Straddle his legs, and wiggle your bottom. Grind slowly and seductively to the music, stroking your breasts, and making eye contact. Then mambo your way over to the mattress.

SUNDAY
Pour yourself into a sexy negligee and refuse to take it off (think of it as the reverse strip). He has to lick and kiss you through the fabric.

A-SEX-ORIZE

How to dress for quickie sex. Being in a state of readiness
will show him you're up for it any time, day or night.

- Stay semi-clothed. If you're prepared to get naked, you're not
  impatient enough to get into the swing of the quickie. Of
  course, ripping your clothes off is a different story.

- Wear a suspender (garter) belt to work, you naughty thing.
  It'll give him easy access later. No tights – unless you have
  a run in a strategic spot!

- Slip into something new. According to one survey, husbands
  who fail to notice that their wives changed their hair colour
  from black to blonde literally leapt to attention at the sight of
  a fresh-off-the-rack pair of lace underpants or an unfamiliar
  push-up bra.

- Forget fashion and slip into a longish skirt – it's ideal for hiking
  up and making a quick discreet connection in public places.

- If you can't skip knickers altogether, make them edible. See
  resources on page 254–5 for where to buy flavoured panties.

- A sexy teddy or leotard that opens at the crotch will have you
  ready in a snap.

- Y-fronts or boxer shorts for him – both were designed with
  a quickie in mind.

SEX UP YOUR LOVE NEST

All it takes is a few small changes to turn your home into an erotic playground of sensual delights.

COME CLEAN

Light a few candles and fill a tub with hot water just before your lover gets home. Nothing says pampered like being bathed. Just don't forget the aphrodisiacs! Perfume the water with scented oils. Studies have found banana and vanilla to be powerful dirty-thoughts triggers.

EAT IN

Instead of your standard takeaway-and-TV evening, make a bedroom picnic treat – complete with a blanket on the floor or spread over the bed. Open a bottle of wine and serve up some simple finger foods like sushi or dim sum (extra points if you can feed each other with chopsticks).

Smooth Move: White wine or champagne is less of a stain hazard than red wine.

MAKE YOUR BED

Few words are sexier than "high thread count". If you want to spend more time in bed, pick up a new sheet set with a thread count of 200 or more, in Turkish or Egyptian cotton. Add plush, velvety blankets.

Smooth Move: Keep the colour scheme simple to appeal to both sexes – no mix-and-match patterns and Marie Antoinette ruffles for her and no tiger patterns or sport logos for him.

ADD A SPRITZ

Lighten up the scents in your home come springtime with lighter, more floral aromas. Sprinkle your sheets with lavender water or rose petals for a special romantic day. Keep the richer, warmer scents like vanilla or musk for winter months. Essential-oil-infused candles or oil diffusers that rest on your lamp bulb will send gentle drifts of calming or sensual scent throughout the room.

LIGHTEN THE MOOD

Stark, super-bright overhead lights make a harsh background for romping. Make sure bulbs are low wattage, keep pink-toned bulbs in bedside lamps to give skin a sexy hue or skip the modern technology altogether and light some scented candles. Cluster just one or two candles on a surface that's at eye level when you're standing. That way, the light will bounce off the ceiling, casting more flattering shadows

Watch Out 1: If you place candles below or at the same height as the bed, they'll cast unflattering shadows – the same way a torch under your chin makes you look like something out of a horror flick.

MAKE BEAUTIFUL SHEET MUSIC TOGETHER

Keep a small sound system near the bed with all your favourite CDs at your fingertips.

Smooth Move: Hearing some overpaid singer crooning about love is not an aphrodisiac, so pick your music carefully. Soothing noises, such as a nature CD, spiritual music or a sound machine, help you to get out of your own head.

GET PHYSICAL

Limber your love muscles – taut muscles make for better sex. According to the American Association of Sex Educators, Counsellors and Therapists, toning your pubococcygeus (that's PC to you) muscles helps lube and stimulate you, making your orgasms come on more quickly and more intensely (this goes for men too). Simply practising a few simple sexercises can boost your level of nookie fitness to the point where your orgasms are more frequent, more intense and longer-lasting. Here's a Six-Day booty camp for how to train – without setting foot in the gym.

DAY ONE: WORKING YOUR PC

No matter how many times you work out a week, no matter how many crunches you can do in one sitting and no matter how much weight you can lift, you'll never work the muscles that really count in sex: the pubococcygeus (PC) muscles. These are a group of muscles on the underside of your body, running from your pubic bone to your tailbone.

A woman with strong PCs can grasp her partner's penis and play with it by contracting and releasing her muscles, taking lovemaking beyond everyday sex and into the territory of the Kama Sutra. A man with taut PCs can be master of his own erections, making them come and stay for as long as he wants. Without exercise, the PCs are flabby.

You can squeeze while commuting to work, waiting in a line or lying on the sofa watching television. As long as you can keep that goofy smile off your face, no one will know what you're squeezing.

For all its payoff, working the PCs actually requires very little effort. To get up to speed, squeeze the muscles that control your pee flow. Try to keep your legs slightly apart rather than clamping your thighs together as you squeeze. Aim to do this 20 times, at approximately one squeeze per second, exhaling gently as you tighten. Don't bear down when you release; simply let go. Do two sets every day, gradually building up to two sets of 75.

For gold-standard love muscles, do the long squeeze: Hold the muscle contraction for a count of three. Relax between contractions. Work up to holding the squeeze for 10 seconds and relaxing for 10 seconds. Again, start with two sets of 20 each and gradually build up to 75.

Crank It Up For Her: Weights designed to exercise the PC muscles in women are available in sex-toy shops. The most common varieties are smooth eggs in varying sizes made of polished wood or stone and tiny barbells. Using her PCs, she pulls the toy into the vagina and pushes it back out.

Continue for one week, then try the following five moves and feel the difference.

PC Move 1

To get the full benefit of his rock-hard PCs, he should tighten them just as he is a groan away from making an extended moan while breathing deeply. This will help him stand to attention for as long as he wants. Eventually, he will have trained to the point where he can climax without ejaculating. Meanwhile, she flexes her PC muscles in time with his thrusting.

PC Move 2

He lies on his back and she lies on top of him with her knees bent. Resting on his chest, she squeezes his penis and slowly circles her hips five times, after which she stops and squeezes. She then squeezes hard again and rotates her hips in the other direction. Continue this cycle until you are both thoroughly aroused.

PC Move 3

He lies on his back, she lies on top of him, face down, with her head by his feet. She should then squeeze her way up and down his pole, making sure each contraction is very powerful. For full effect, she should briefly pause between squeezes.

PC Move 4

He sits up and she squats on him. You both thrust towards each other ten times and then stop and squeeze your PCs ten times.

PC Move 5

He lies on top of her and, instead of going at her like a pneumatic drill, he stays inside her, lying like a dog playing dead. Then he squeezes and releases his PC muscle. She returns the squeeze until it feels like your love organs are giving each other hugs.

DAY TWO: REMEMBER TO BREATHE

Use this technique before or during lovemaking to get in the groove. Keeping your mouth closed, take rapid, rhythmic and shallow breaths through the nose. Breathe this way for one to three minutes. There's no simpler way to oxygenate the blood, a course of action that powers sexual energy and ignites desire.

DAY THREE: BUILDING A BETTER MACHINE

Turn your body into a love machine. The three areas you use most during sex (other than your love muscles, of course) are your arms, back and your glutes.

Arms

You need arms of steel for lifting, thrusting and sustained vibrator-hoisting. Work out your biceps, triceps and forearms all at once by sitting down on a chair and grabbing either side of the seat. Slide your bottom forwards so it's just in front of the chair, then lower your body 15–25 cm (6–10 in). Slowly rise back up, keeping your back straight and flush against the front of the chair. Do as many reps as you can, then rest for 30 seconds. That's a set. Do three sets.

Back

In almost every sex position, your back supports most of your body's weight. To strengthen it, stand facing the side of a chair and put your left knee and left hand on the seat close to the chair back so your right arm can hang down with the weight of your right hand. Support yourself with your right leg and slightly bend your right knee. Your back should be parallel with the floor. Grab an object that weighs 4–7 kg (10–15 lb) – a dumbbell or the dog – with your right hand. Starting with your arm hanging straight down, pull the weight up to chest height. Repeat as many times as you can, then switch to the other side. Do three sets on each side.

Glutes

Tighten the muscles in your bottom and you'll be able to thrust more powerfully. To powerhorse your rear bumpers, stand with your feet shoulder-width apart, hold in that gut of yours and bend your knees until your thighs are parallel with the floor. Keep your back straight and lean forwards slightly, as if you were sitting down on a toilet, then straighten your legs again. Complete two sets of 15.

DAY FOUR: WORK IT

You have the motivation but wish you had more the time to make Day Three's set of drills a regular part of your life routine? Or maybe you're wishing that working out could bring you as much pleasure as sex? Wish no more. These ten moves count not only as great sex, but also great exercise. Get ready to do victory laps.

The Press Down (works the shoulders)

She lies face up underneath him. He penetrates and then moves up and down by doing press-ups (push-ups) that are about half the range of movement of standard ones. While he is inside her, he needs to keep his body stiff like a board and his hands planted firmly down. Switch positions so she also gets a work out.

Crank It Up: At the bottom of each rep, he should dip his hips to get deeper penetration.

The Push Back (works the triceps)

She sits with her hands on the floor behind her – fingers pointed forwards – and leans back, supporting her weight on her arms. He slips between her thighs with his knees and hands on the floor, his head just over her shoulder. She lifts her bottom off the ground. Once he lowers himself onto (and into) her, she does the work. From a bent-elbow starting position, she thrusts towards him by straightening her arms and then bending them again. For more tension, he can lean against her until she's supporting most of his weight. Switch positions so he also gets a work out.

Love Curls (works the biceps)

She stands about 1 m (3 ft) from the wall, facing forwards. She leans her lower back and shoulders against the wall. He lies against her with his chest to hers, his legs pressed against her, his dumbbell inside of her. She scoops her arms around so her hands are resting against his shoulder blades. He leans back until her arms are extended (taking care he doesn't slip out). She slowly curls him back to her. To make it easier, he can put his arms around her and help pull himself up. Switch positions so he also gets a work out.

The Body Bend (works the upper back)

With her back to him, her knees bent and leaning forwards slightly, she plants her legs firmly with feet about 46 cm (18 in) apart. He drapes himself over her and moves in from behind. Placing her hands on her upper thighs, she supports his weight, using her upper back to move you both up and down.

Single Squat (works the glutes, hamstrings and bottom)

He lies flat and she squats over him with her feet flat on the floor. Without otherwise touching, she lowers herself so his arrow sinks into her bull's eye. She then lifts herself to the point where he almost bows out of position, before plunging down again. He can fiddle with her other playthings as she moves up and down.

Double Squat (works the quads and hamstrings)

He squats low, leaning back against a wall. She squats over him, making sure she keeps her knees bent at a right angle. She moves up and down on his penis by pressing with her thighs.

Smooth Move: If this is too hard, she can give him some of her weight by putting her hands on his thighs.

Lift Up (works the glutes)

Kneeling in the missionary/man-on-top (see page 100) position he supports her by slipping his hands under her hips and lifting her pelvis up while she clenches her tush muscles.

Crunches (works the abs)

Her lower abdomen, just above the pubic hairline, is basically the outside of the inner clitoris, so squeezing the ab muscles intensifies the feeling while tightens the tummy. He kneels in missionary (see page 100) and she does a mini sit-up during sex, sandwiching her inner clitoris between two hard surfaces (her muscles and his penis).

Smooth Move: Make sure his penis is in place before she starts crunching.

Thigh Press (works the inner and outer thighs)
Lying on top of him, she opens and closes her legs during sex in small pumps.

Crank It Up: The tighter she squeezes, the more friction she will cause on her clitoris and the inner folds of the vulva, which are rich in nerve endings.

Love Muscle Squeeze (works the penis)
She stands facing him and grasps the muscle in one hand. She should then massage it in a firm but gentle up-down motion. Repeat. Repeat. Repeat …

DAY FIVE: SEXTREME ORGASMS
Now that you've mastered basic training, you can try some advanced techniques. These are not for couch potatoes.

Body Lift
She gets on all fours on the floor. He enters her from behind. He then wraps his arms around her thighs as he stands up (he should look like he is pushing a wheelbarrow).

Smooth Move 1: He should push in as deep as possible.

Smooth Move 2: She walks around on her hands, with him thrusting as they go.

Buckin' Bronco
He sits on the bed with his legs extended in front of him and knees bent. She sits on his lap and lowers herself onto his erect penis with her feet flat on the bed. She then leans back with her hands on the bed for support.

Crank It Up 1: She straddles his lap with her knees on the floor, and then leans into a backbend (being careful not to strain her lower back).

Crank It Up 2: She then leans back fully to rest the top of her head on the bed and reaches back with her hands until they grasp his feet.

Gymnast
She stands facing her partner with her left foot turned out and her right foot forwards. His legs should be slightly bent, spaced about 1 m (3 ft) apart. With her arms on his shoulders and his arms around her lower back, she slowly pulls her right leg up and props her right foot on his left shoulder. After he sinks his putt, she eases into a vertical split by sliding her calf as far up his left shoulder as she comfortably can.

Tree
Start with him sitting on a chair. Facing him, she lowers herself onto his erect penis until she's sitting on his lap. While she wraps her arms and legs tightly around him, he cradles her lower back and bottom while he slowly stands up.

Smooth Move: Propping her back up against a wall for support or resting her rear end on a table will make this move easier for him.

Crank It Up: If he's been working his moves for Days 1–3, he should be strong enough to lift her up and down on his penis.

Plough
She lies on her back and lifts her legs so they're over her ears and parallel to the floor. He kneels in front of her, butting his knees against her lower back to support her. He leans his body up against her thighs, dips in and gently rocks them both back and forth.

Smooth Move: She can hold his legs in place.

Trapeze
She lies on her back on a bed with her legs spread apart slightly. He kneels in front of her and places the backs of her knees in the crooks of his elbows. He then pulls upward so that her lower back and bottom are raised off the bed at a 20- to 30-degree angle and the backs of her thighs are pressed against his stomach and chest. He should be able to enter her easily this way, as her bottom will be cupped between his quads with her love muscle pressing right up against his.

Smooth Move: Use one or more pillows beneath her tush and back to hike her up and give her more to yahoo about.

Watch Out: He will need good balance or you will end up toppling like a house of cards.

DAY SIX: RUB DOWN

Soothe those sore muscles with an erotic massage. All you need is some vegetable oil (sunflower, safflower or coconut) and a coin to toss to decide who goes first. The person receiving (called Lucky Bastard from now on) lies flat on their back. The person massaging (hereafter known as Slave) rubs a couple of tablespoons of oil between their palms to warm it up. The Slave then sits astride the Lucky Bastard's tummy and using long gliding strokes, rubs the oil into their chest, neck, shoulders and arms. They should use more oil as they need it. The Slave then moves their chest over the Lucky Bastard's, lightly brushing them with their nipples, moving side to side and up and down. The Slave then opens the Lucky Bastard's legs and slides between them to gently massage their love muscles until they melt. Next time round, swap roles.

Smooth Move: Add a couple of drops of an essential oil to your vegetable oil. Rosemary, jasmine and ylang ylang are all known instant aphrodisiacs.

Watch Out: If you use latex contraceptive, use lotion instead of oil as your massage grease.

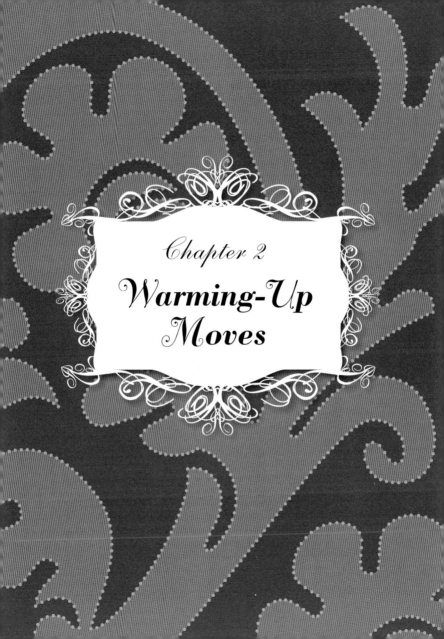

Chapter 2
Warming-Up Moves

FIVE KISSING TIPS

Kissing isn't as easy as it looks. There's an art to it, and clamping your lips together and hoping for the best isn't it. Here are five gotta-have-it-now lip locks to lay on each other right now. Pucker up!

1 Alternate between deep teeth-gnashing, lip-bruising French kisses (for him) and light, feathery kisses (for her).

2 Don't just go mouth-to-mouth. Throw your whole body into it. Cradle his face with one hand and grab his bottom with the other while grinding your breasts and pelvis against him.

3 While making out, wrap your lips around his tongue and suck, starting slow and soft and gradually building up to fast and stiff. It'll feel like you're making love to his mouth.

4 Kiss each other some sweet place you never have before.

5 Tug his bottom lip with your teeth, lightly suck his tongue when it's in your mouth. Nibble at his neck and tickle the roof of his mouth with your tongue

TEN KAMA SUTRA KISSING TIPS

Kissing is as intimate a deed as the actual act of sex itself. Here's now to make mouth magic the Eastern way.

1 Get seduction going with a Bent Kiss – your heads angle towards each other and your lips connect very gently.

2 Turn on by kissing Turned Style. Reach out, and while cradling your lover's chin, turn their face up towards you.

3 For an oh-so-hot smooch give it to him straight on – lock lips without touching any other part of his body.

4 Get a tingly sensation by giving him a Clasping Kiss. Take both his lips between your own and nibble gently (In the original Kama Sutra, a woman only bestows this kiss on a man with no moustache – perhaps because the hairs would get caught in her mouth!)

5 Make him drool with a Greatly Pressed Kiss. Take hold of the lower lip between two fingers and, after caressing it with your tongue, strongly press your lips against it. Crank things up a notch by licking the rim of each other's lips and get your whole body into the action of making out by grabbing his butt while you grind against him.

6 For a passionate, gotta-have-it-now lip lock do the Fight With Your Tongues. Tease him by tracing the outside of his lips with your tongue, gently tugging his bottom lip with your teeth, and lightly biting his tongue whenever it's in your mouth.

7 Try Tantric kisses. Sweeten your kisses by sucking each other's lips as you concentrate on breathing in tandem.

8 Plant light kisses all over his face while he's asleep; this is known as the Kiss That Kindles Love.

9 Make your smooches feel like oral sex by tugging on his tongue. Because the tongue muscle is connected to the throat, you actually end up stimulating the muscles in his neck and chest with this move – so one kiss will work his whole torso.

10 Go public with your love on the quiet. When you're out in the world, present your finger (when you're standing) or your toe (if you're sitting) for him to feast upon.

TIT-ELATION

It's a fact: 99.99% of men are obsessed by breasts. But true tit-elation is when all it takes are a few bust-out moves to make those mounds quiver.

- For breast in show, slip into a pushup bra. Strut your stuff and watch him howl like a dog.

- Make a sandwich by slipping his hotdog between your top buns and moving gently from side to side while he thrusts back and forth. For extra juice, add a squirt of lube. The friction will make him ask for seconds.

- Adorn your breast self – see page 203 and Resources on pages 254–5 for what the best boobs are wearing these days, such as nipple rings, chains and clamps. Or slip on a front-opening bra, straddle him and then pop the girls out onto his waiting mouth.

- Skip the nipple. The top, bottom and sides of your breasts are actually where all the ultrasensitive nerve action is.

INSTANT TURN-ONS
Memorize the following phrases and use at your own carnal risk.

- Caress your lover's cheek, lock eyes and utter three simple words: "I want you."

- Any email longer than "CU later" will keep you on each other's brains all day and make it easier to slip into some one-on-one action when you are F2F.

- Scream, "Boo". Scaring each other stimulates the neurotransmitter dopamine in the brain, which in turn can trigger your sex drive.

- Saying "I don't need to answer that" if your mobile or pager goes off while you're together guarantees an orgasm later.

Pick up a pair of furry handcuffs (available from sex shops like www.annsummers.com, www.libida.com and www. sh-womenstore.com) and pass them to him under the table at a restaurant, saying "Here's a little something for later." He'll be asking for the bill before you finish your sentence.

Cooking together heats up more than the kitchen. Whip up an easy sophisticated cheesy snack (sauté asparagus stalks in olive oil for three minutes, sprinkle with Parmesan, salt and pepper) that's packed with zinc, a key mineral needed for getting and staying lusty. Add a clove of crushed garlic if you want to boost blood flow to special places. Follow with a wicked chocolate dessert and you'll load up on phenylethylamine, a neurotransmitter that activates the brain's pleasure centre, and caffeine, which can jolt your sex drive. Start feasting.

Put on lipstick in front of him. He'll start fantasizing about your lips and what he wants them to do. Better yet, let him put it on your lips for you. Caress the tresses. Each hair follicle has its own sensitive nerve. Sink your fingers in, lightly pull the shafts up and away from the scalp and they'll feel it right down to their curling toes.

GETTING YOURSELF READY FOR ACTION

You can only speed things up so much. Study after study shows that women need at least 15 minutes of foreplay before they're good and ready to move on both mentally and physically (in addition to having do-me-now urges, she needs to start lubricating and her vaginal canal must expand to handle his – er – abundance). These five moves will rev your engine. Don't be shy – most men are willing and eager to do whatever it takes to please their bedfellow.

- Pick up some female-friendly porn like the *Black Lace* or *X Libris* series to read together. Besides getting you hot under the collar, the torrid prose will give him lots of sizzling ideas for bawdy things he can try with you.

- He can send you into a tailspin simply by spiralling his fingertips along your forearms, neck, the palms of your hands and any other sensitive body spot. The circular motion is much more intense than the usual up-and-down straight line rub.

- When in doubt, kiss. Women get immense erotic pleasure from frequent, lusty, passionate make-out sessions. Just remember that this does not always mean frantically wrestling tongues. Try to mix up your lip play with the occasional oh-so-seductive butterfly peck on the nose, eyes, forehead and other body parts.

- For a heart-racing sensation, have him almost-caress you by holding his fingertips just above your skin and running his hands over your naked arms, breasts, belly and thighs so they just brush those fine body hairs. Mmmm.

- Don't beat around the bush about requesting oral. It's the shortest, fastest route to paradise for most women (a fluent cunnilinguist can bring a woman to orgasm in minutes).

USE YOUR SENSES

IF IT TASTES GOOD...

Indulge in a tasty turn-on. Lay cuddling in side-to-side and slip berries or pieces of mango back and forth between your mouths.

Bite me. There's nothing more erotic than a partner who knows where and how to give love bites. He can nibble at her shoulders and neck when he drapes his body over yours and slips in from behind. You can reciprocate as you cosy up during afterplay.

Watch Out: Don't bite so hard that you leave identifying tooth marks.

IF IT SOUNDS GOOD...

The Sounds of Seduction: You lie flat and he gets on top. You should relax your vaginal muscles as he goes up and tighten them on the downswing. With practise, you'll make a loud, sexy, squishy sound.

Heartbeat: You're on top of him. After orgasm, stretch out so you're lying flat on his body. The sound of his heartbeat will reverberate through your body.

Triple-X Story Hour: Take turns getting on top and reading erotic stories to each other – whoever is in the upper position sits and reads.

Smooth Move: A good source of erotica for him-and-her is anything by Susie Bright.

Surround Yourself With Sexy Sounds

- So you want a little foul-mouthed foreplay? Good. But it's only sexy talk if you're speaking the same language. Sit opposite each other, point to your bits and decide together what you're going to call them. Clothing optional.

- When it comes to making sheet music together, some tunes rap out a sexier beat than others. Any number that has you toe-tapping faster than the human heartbeat (about 72 RPMs) will arouse your doin'-it desires while slow-beat scores like those found in reggae, Latin or Barry White songs will send good vibrations throbbing through your lower body.

- Talk in public. Plant yourself in a crowded place (on a blanket in a park, at a club or party, in a busy restaurant) and whisper your fantasies to one another, sparing no racy detail. You can do something about it later, when you get home.

- Let the foreplay begin on your drive home. Call your lover and say you've been thinking all day about having a passionate, steamy encounter with him. Or tell him you'll meet him at a specific time in the bedroom with no clothes on.

IF IT SMELLS GOOD...

Heaven Scent
The nose is connected to the limbic system of the brain, which controls libido. So certain scents – rose, jasmine and ylang ylang – can trigger sexual arousal. Rub a couple of drops of scented oil (available at health-food outlets) into each other's love areas. Then he lies on his back with a pillow propped under his head. Facing him, lower yourself onto his member and puts your hands and knees on either side of his torso. Once he's deep inside, move gently to the left, then down, right, and up. You'll literally be grinding the sexy scents into the air, turning your loveplay into a heady affair.

Smooth Move: Sniff deeply.

Watch Out: Don't do this move using latex contraception as the oils will melt down your protection.

Scent-ualize Your Loveplay

- Take a bath together in scented water.

- Make sure your breath is fresh – sausage and beer fumes will make your partner keel over.

- Light a scented candle to let loose a sexy aroma and get rid of any stinky smells in the air, which can be a turn-off.

IF IT LOOKS GOOD...

Tantric Gazing: Plug into each other with a little eye arousal. Lie facing each other with his penis barely inside you. Gaze into each other's eyes for a full minute or two before he plunges all the way in. By locking eyes, you reach a deep level of intimacy that is incredibly hot and makes sex really intense.

Eye to Eye: Sitting straight up on top of him gives you a full-eye view of each other.

Crank It Up: Jiggle about so that he can watch your breasts play bouncy.

Spread Eagle: Take turns being tied spread-eagle to the bed. Turn out the lights. Then use a torch and let it play over your lover's body, highlighting each part and telling them in great detail exactly what you are going to do to that part. Then do it.

Sight-ualize Your Loveplay

- Remember to look at each other during the deed to tune in to what your lover is feeling – and needing – at the moment.

- Check out a sexy flick together for an appetizer turn-on.

- Even better, take snaps of each other in sexy poses.

SENSUAL MASSAGE

To get primed for a down-and-dirty divine time, squeeze a few drops of scented oil in your hands and place them on your lover's thigh just above their knee. Gently knead the thighs, making your way north and building the sexual tension. When you get to the groin area, work the muscles around the private parts, but don't actually touch anything that counts. Take turns repeating this on each other before slipping into a classic 69 with him on the bottom with your head between his legs. This is the most comfortable position to let you both pleasure each other while flying high on the aromas.

> **Watch Out:** If you slide into actual intercourse, don't mix oil and latex contraception.

LOVE IN THE DARK

Blindfold each other and feel your way. Not knowing where you'll be touched next can heighten sexual tension, and there's something about being unable to see that makes your other senses respond more intensely. When you can't take it any more, he can roll on top (the easiest position to slip into blind).

YOUR OWN PRIVATE PEEP SHOW

You don't even need to touch him. Just seeing you do some sexy thing injects an instant shot of testosterone into his bloodstream. Put him on guard by locking eyes with him. Then reach under your shirt, arch and unclasp your bra. Wriggle it free and toss it towards him. As you play, pull back your hair so he can see what's going on and set the action in front of a mirror so you can both watch.

STROKES AND CARESSES

When it comes to foreplay, men and women crave distinctly different finger moves. Women get turned on by softer, gentler caresses while men typically want things hard and harder. Take turns giving each other a sensuous gender-customized stroking. He can use a feather to lightly trace tingly touches over your skin while you can limber up your hands with oil to give him a deep penetrating rubdown all over his body.

There are parts of your body that are so seldom touched that they are, by default, especially sensitive. Discover yours by touching each other using any part of your body – your hair, your feet, your lips – except your hands.

AVOID THESE TOUCHY-FEELY MOVES:

• Scratching anywhere near his boys with inch-long talons.

• Rubbing him down with patchouli, rose, jasmine or any other girlie-scented oil.

• Pinching, punching or anything that will leave bruises.

• Jamming his boner so hard it cracks.

Warning: Some of these body parts don't often see the light of day so make sure they all pass the sniff test (wield a washcloth behind the ears, the belly button, underarms, the top crease of the bottom and the toes). According to a study, good grooming counts even higher than penis or breast size with some lovers!

TAKE A STEAMY SHOWER TOGETHER
… with the lights out. For extra shower power, make it a threesome.

Pour a couple of drops of shower gel into a spray bottle and mix it with water. Spray each other, then rub. You'll feel three different types of stimulation – the steady pelting of the shower, the soft spray of the soapy gel and the firm caresses of your lover's mitts.

PLAY IN THE ZONE
Getting as close to tried-and-trues without actually touching them will make you wiggle and wriggle for more. By the time you actually cross over their erogenous borders, the sensation will be that much more earth-shaking.

- To release endorphins and get your lover in the mood, use your tongue or finger to lightly probe the ultra-sensitive skin behind the ear. Stimulate the auriculogenital reflex (ear-stimulation response) by heavy breathing into the ear. Some people find it so exciting they actually climax from it.

- Men's neck skin tends to be thicker, so use your whole mouth to suck on his skin. Or alternate sucking with gently biting a path up and down his neck. If you want to leave your mark, suck in one spot hard. Ambidextrous vampires can use their tongues to caress and soothe the bruised skin at the same time.

- The area between the belly button and pubic bone is packed with pleasure points. To arouse them all, massage, lick or nibble the soft skin from the navel down to where the pubic hair begins. Take turns sitting erect on the edge of a chair with the other person standing behind. The one standing places their hands in a triangle on the sitter's abdomen, pointing downward, and rubs. The person on the receiving end will soon feel a sexy buzz building up.

- The inner thighs are ultra-quivering to touch. They're also the home of the lymphatic system, which releases chemicals that cleanse the body of toxins. Which is why kneading a handful of the soft flesh in this area can create a pleasant buzzy state.

- Using both hands, start at the hips and caress the flesh working your way toward the inner thighs. Now trace the same line with your mouth. Repeat this alternating sexy build-up until he can't take it any more (you'll know because he'll push your head toward a more central between-the-legs region).

- Give his tootsies a soaking by gently sucking the toes, from the big one down to the little one. Finish with a tongue swirl over the hyper-responsive in-step.

WATCH PORN

Not only is this a great warm-up prelude to sex, it'll also give you some insider info to the opposite sex. But it will not produce the desired results (white-hot blinding lust) if your naughty video of choice features a seriously clueless bimbo, who keeps getting banged by big men out of the blue or lots of naked men and women sitting around talking. Pick a couple of friendly flicks (check out the user-friendly rating system at www.goodvibrations.com and www.evesgarden.com). Watch it with the sound turned off – it's actually hotter when you lose the stilted horny workman/smutty housewife dialogue.

SHAKE THINGS UP

Some vibrators shake, rattle, roll and even lick. But if you're shopping for the dream his-'n'-her machine, opt for something that fits in the palm of your hand, such as a finger vibrator, mini bullet or pocket rocket. It'll produce the same power vibes as a mega version without freaking out either of you over its size.

Don't get lazy: It's not just that little guy by himself but the sexy combo of you and your battery-operated mate that sends your partner into seventh (or even eighth) heaven. Here are four ways to work together to get the best orgasmic results.

1 Run the vibrator over your partner's nipples while you concentrate on licking below.

2 Team up down under – alternate using your mouth and your buzzing buddy.

3 Make it feel like an orgy by working your other hand into the mix.

4 Rub the vibrator along parts of their body that you don't usually think of as sexy and see how fast you revise your opinion.

RAISING (AND LOWERING) THE TEMPERATURE
Playing with temperatures can make lukewarm lovemaking sizzle.

• Blow. Warm breath on the skin raises its temperature. Head for less obvious thin-skinned spots like the earlobes, neck and inner thighs.

• Work up a slow burn by gently massaging a small blob of heat-activated lube (check out Resources on pages 254–5 for where to buy) all over his penis. The longer you rub, the warmer it gets.

• Sip some hot water, but don't swallow. Instead, carefully swallow him. The heated liquid will bring him to boiling point.

• Dribble warmed-up (finger-test the temperature first) honey, chocolate or syrup over their body and lick off.

Adding a frosty touch to your foreplay can actually make things hotter because it energizes your nerve cells. Here's how to add thrills with chills...

• Ice him. After working his body into a sweat, run an ice cube from his neck all the way down one side of his body, up the inside of his leg (but staying away from his heat stick), down the other side and back up.

- Crank the mercury back up to heatwave numbers by doing the above, but hold the ice cube in your hot little mouth this time.

- Fill a condom with water and freeze. Peel off the condom and hey presto, you have a dildo lolly to play with.

- Blow hot and cold. Done in succession, these two sensations pack a one-two wallop to your orgasms. The easiest way is to lick a small area and then blow hot air on the wet patch. Even better is to use booze because the alcohol evaporates more quickly than water, so it creates a cooler effect when you blow.

PLAYING ROUGH

Get hard on him. He's the stronger sex, so he can take it. Pinch his nipples (an often-overlooked nerve centre), scratch your nails down his back, massage his chest, knead his bottom, squeeze his boy parts. He'll get off on your girl-gone-wild manhandling.

BLIND LOVE

Grab a scarf and play Rock, Paper, Scissors to decide who gets blindfolded first. The giver should take their time. Mix up where your hands and mouth strike next to dangle your lover on the edge of ecstasy for as long as possible.

HOTTING IT UP
Three games for playing ball with him.

1 Don't just grease up his bat. Squirt some lube between your hands and gently rub it all around his testicles.

2 Wrestle his testicles into joyful submission by gently tugging on them.

3 Get him to sit up and beg by using your finger to lightly scratch the underside of his balls.

FINGER PLAY
Have him give you the finger. This is the best move for pushing your G-spot (a soft swelling that lives halfway up the front wall of your vagina that will make you scream with joy when pressed). He should slide his thumb up about 5 cm (2 in) and press hard as if he were trying to make a thumbprint on the front of your vaginal wall.

Say Aaaah! Studies show that merely finger stroking your anterior fornix zone (located on the front wall of the vagina between the G-spot and the cervix) can juice you up and multiple orgasms.

Get bummed. That tiny little hole is actually crammed with spine-tingling nerves. You don't have to go in deep; a well-lubed finger pressing around the outer regions is all it takes to cause a melt-down. If you do want to go in further, make sure your fingers and the entire area are clean and well-lubed.

BEG-FOR-MERCY MANOEUVRES

While men and women aren't from different planets, simple biology confirms that we are not made on the same basic model. So what gets his motor revving might not have the same turn-on effect for you. Perfect these beg-for-mercy manoeuvres, and he'll never want to get out of bed.

1 Show yourself. Men like to see naked women. That's why they like porn. This doesn't meant you have to slap on nipple tassels and perform a strip act (though that would do it). Simply leave the lights on during sex.

2 Show him your inner guy and spit on him. Unlike women, men don't have built-in lubricants. You can stroke it dry, but you may as well suggest a session of carpet burns for all the pleasure it will give him. Saliva is your best lubricant, so give your hand a big sexy lick.

3 Show him that you know his body better than he knows it himself. Many men aren't aware of the range of erotic areas on their bodies.

Surprise him: instead of directing most of your attention to what's below his belt try these:

• His ears – poking in and out with a wet tongue makes him go crazy, especially if you breath a little dirty talk into the mix.

• The back of his neck. Just lightly scratching his neck using small circular movements is extremely exciting for him.

- His nipples. These are exclamation points for him – make them shout with a little kissing and caressing. The more pressure you use, the better.

- His lower belly. This is like an oasis stop on the way down to the penis. Licking it or even tracing your finger over the area will make him stand and quiver to attention.

- His bum. As much as he likes you paying attention to the doorpull at the front, he likes your hands to wander around to the backdoor occasionally to make his thighs feel naughty and oh-sooooo nice.

FAIR PLAY

**His 'n' her get-busy-in-a-jiffy basics that'll deliver mind-blowing
results. Yes, you could just speed ahead to grabbing his penis
and pulling to turn him on. But it's so much more fun for him
(and you) to dally in the slow lane. Here are four slow-mo
moves that might get him arrested for sexually loitering.**

1 Get him to take a deep breath. Whatever activity he's
attempting (World Championship Ironman or your own
personal iron man), deep, regulated breathing will help him
stay in control without losing his will. When he feels like he's
burning out, he should stay very still, relax his genital muscles,
and take a long breath in through his nose for a count of five
seconds and hold it for two before slowly exhaling through
his mouth for six seconds. He'll be able to stay in peak
condition for as long as you want to play.

2 Go ahead and bring him to the brink. Then ignore him. It's a
guaranteed way to send him into a frenzy... and swell his
orgasm later.

3 Trick him. Get very close to his naughty bits with your mouth
and then pass right on by. To really make him twist and burn,
blast some hot air into the area.

4 Indulge your inner dominatrix. Position his body how you
want it or, if he makes a move to head down below, pull him
back up if you're not ready. Being the object of your sexual

attention will bring his entire body to a fever pitch. He doesn't have to ask for what he wants or worry about how he's doing performance-wise. And playing Mistress means you get the kind of stimulation you need, when and where you want it.

PROLONGING FOREPLAY

Not ready to call an end to your play? Try these tricks to get him to stay in the game for as long as you want.

- Add a chill – such as an ice cube or wet towel – against the small of his back to distract him long enough to regain control. Cold shower, anyone?

- If he starts dribbling, let him go. He's reached the point of no return and risks straining or even tearing his urethra in his attempts to squeeze back the flow.

- If he's regularly trigger happy, help him put his safety lock on by holding the shaft of his penis in your hand, firmly squeezing for ten seconds and then releasing.

- Slip on a condom. A love glove helps keep him in check. A desensitizing gel may slow things down, but you risk transferring it and numbing your own happy regions.

- To give him a second wind, lay him down flat. This will stop the blood flow from springing his love gun back into firing stance.

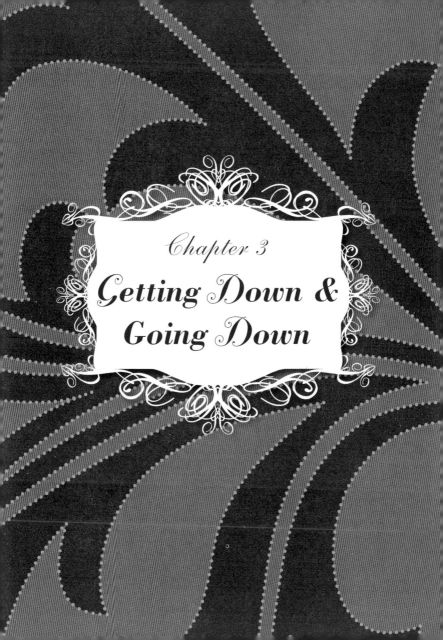

Chapter 3

Getting Down & Going Down

TICKLE HIS PICKLE

Don't make the mistake of thinking oral sex is like footie in that the use of hands is not permitted – you will need back-up and this is where the handjob comes in. If you only use your mouth, you risk dishing out the world's longest blowjob. Not because your mouthwork isn't seductive and steamy, but because most men enjoy (and often need) extra stimulation to intensify and speed up their joyride to bliss. Master these multitasking tips and he'll love you for your carnal coordination. Start with the basics – here are six steps to perfecting your handshake.

1   Get a grip. Which hand do you write with? Then make sure that paw has easy access when you deliver the goods or you may end up with worker's cramp (with no guaranteed compensation).

2   Lick your hand. Unlike women, men don't have built-in lubricants. If you use your new extra-strong grip on him dry, you'll probably give him carpet burn.

3   To perform a workaday, no-frills handjob (which will still plaster a goofy grin on his face), firmly but gently grasp your hand around the base of the penis and slide it upwards until it reaches the head. Then rub your palm over the head in tiny, exquisite circles. Slide your hand back down to base camp and, adjusting your hand so that your palm is squeezing the opposite side of his pole, repeat the move. Continue, making each upward squeeze last at least ten seconds. After every fifth upward squeeze, throw in a quick, firm, up-and-down pump stroke.

4 When in doubt, press even harder. If you're not sure how hard, have him give you a hands-on demo of how he likes to touch himself, and then follow his lead.

5 Once you have the basics down cold, throw these make-his-toes-curl handholds into the mix.

• **The Tickler:** Make his Mr Happy even happier by lightly tracing your fingers over the entire area.

• **The Big Squeeze:** Press your palms flat against the sides of the shaft and press hard while at the same time moving your hands up and down.

• **The Corkscrew:** Squeeze the head of his penis and gently wiggle it back and forth while holding the base with your other hand.

• **The Kneader:** Hold his baguette so that your thumbs are touching. Lightly pull in opposite directions and then come back together.

• **The Ring:** Encircle just below the head of his penis with your thumb and forefinger and pump up and down with it.

Do any of the above in public and he will worship at your feet.

GIVING HIM A HAND

Most women don't have the first idea how to handle a penis. They grab, fumble, then give up. The amount of hands-on pressure that would make you say "Ouch" will very likely make him say "Ooooh, yeah." Men's skin tends to be thicker and their nerve endings aren't as close to the skin's surface as women's are. Use as much pressure as you would when shaking your boss's hand – hard enough to make an impression, but not so hard you leave a dent.

How To: Form a snug fist around the base of his shaft (slathering on some lube makes this manoeuvre slicker and easier). Then glide your hand up his penis, gripping it firmly. Once you reach the top, twist your wrist and open your hand so the flattest part of your palm is resting on the head. Caress it – alternating back-and-forth and circular motions – for just a few moments. Then grip the shaft with your palm around the head, and work downwards with closed fingers. Repeating this wrist-twist trick while upping your speed will take him to the brink of an incredible climax (or push him over the precipice).

MAKE FRIENDS WITH HIS BEST FRIEND
Explore these three hot spots around his genitals

- **The frenulum.** This is the place on the underside of his penis where the foreskin attaches to the head. An ultra-sensitive spot, it's like a male clitoris packed with nerve endings. A little added pressure from your fingers will set off an orgasmic chain reaction.

- **The perineum.** Pressing this little triangle of love nestling between his scrotum and his anus can intensify the level of his orgasms. Try using two fingers for two seconds, and then release. Do it a few times – it'll take him a week to recover.

- **The prostate.** The only way to scratch this baby's backside is to stick a well-lubed finger up his bum (you may want to suit up in latex before you dive in).

GET HIM TO LEND A HAND

1 Get him to button you up by lightly tapping with his tongue or finger on the top of your clitoris while caressing the top of your bottom where the crease ends.

2 Turn his penis into his eleventh finger. Grasp it at the base and slowly rub it over your clitoris. At the same time, reach behind and work your fingers against the rim of each other's rear entries.

3 Get him to give you a full working over inside, outside and through the back. He begins with a sweet circular stroke to your love bud. Once you're feeling fine, he crooks his forefinger into a "come hither" position and slips it inside of you to tap lightly against the G-spot. While tapping, he substitutes his tongue for the finger working your genital blossom. This frees up that hand to gently rotate around your back garden. Don't be surprised if you promise a BJ a day for the rest of his life in the heat of passion.

M&MS (MUTUAL MASTURBATION)

You don't have to let the pleasure stop short with your own hand. Why do you think almost every porno flick has some babe wanking? Because men get off on it. Besides, M&M is the safest sex you can have with someone else – plus you are both guaranteed to get what you want. It's also a good move for when he's not into sex or doesn't have the right touch so you have to take things into your own hands.

You can make the leap from solo to partner masturbation with minimum effort (and maximum orgasmic return). Just put your hand where you want and let the games begin – he might decide to work with you, attend to his own needs or sit back and watch. Polish yourself off and hopefully he'll get the hint that it's okay to do the same. Or tell him you like to watch (and then do – it's probably the best way to find out what really makes him yodel).

PERFORMING LIP SERVICE

Here's a little secret: The reason he rates blowjobs so highly is because to him your mouth feels like your vagina with a brain. Depending on where his penis hails from, he may still be wearing a turtleneck (America is one of the few countries where the men are circumcised for nonreligious reasons). The foreskin (a loose fold of skin that covers the glans or the head of the penis) doesn't always stretch back and allow full access once he's erect, so check out the uncut version of the tip for getting under his hood.

A little enthusiasm goes a long way. More than an incredible body or a great technique, what gets him going is knowing that you truly want his penis in your mouth. So before you even get near his fly, let him know how thrilled you are to get on kissing terms with his little guy and not just doing charity work ("Please, please can I go down on you?"). Contrary to urban legend, most men take longer than a boiled egg to get off. Expect to spend at least 10 minutes down there.

However you arrange yourselves, never force a good penis down once he's up. Putting downward pressure on an erect penis strains the suspensory ligaments, the two long tendons that give him the wherewithal to become stiff in the first place. Stretched too far, they'll lose their spring which will result in an erection that may permanently point down instead of up. The key is to strike a pose that has him moving upward into your mouth. Read on for a slant on the top four pole positions you can take.

THE CALL GIRL

One of the most popular moves, he stands up or kneels and you crouch between his legs with your head at the level of his crotch.

Ups: You get plenty of freedom of movement to show off your stuff.

Downs: He can control the thrust and depth. Put your hand at base to stay in the driver's seat.

THE 69

This is a great position where you can both give and receive at the same time by lying down facing each other with your heads at opposite ends (variations on the theme: he's on top and you're on bottom, vice versa or you lie side by side).

Ups: You get as good as you give.

Downs: Since you're both caught up in your own blissfest, you never get or give all that much. Much better is to do a 69 where you take turns taking care of each other.

LYING DOWN, PART ONE

He's flat on his back and you're kneeling over him.

Ups: You are in total control.

Downs: None, actually.

LYING DOWN, PART TWO

You're flat on your back and he's ducking and diving over you.

Ups: He gets plenty of feel-good depth.

Downs: He gets plenty of feel-good depth. Try lying with your head slightly hanging over the edge of bed. While he essentially stays in control of the thrusting, your throat will now be opened wide enough to be able to take him in without gagging (plus it looks porn-star sexy).

SITTING

He lounges on a chair or sofa with you next to him, bent over his bounty.

Ups: This is a good position for a relative beginner as the limited range of movement means he can't thrust up into your mouth.

Downs: You can't take that much in your mouth once you become more adept. Change positions so that you're kneeling between his legs instead of bowing over them.

BLOWJOB BASICS

Don't worry if he's as flabby as an old lady's triceps when you start your play. You'll get his penis into a hardbody lickety split with these buff moves. A word of caution before you begin: Wait until he's fully ready to play before starting the heavy tackles. If he thrusts his penis before it is fully erect, he risks bending-and-buckling injuries, which could end up benching him for the season at best and possibly leaving him with a painfully perpetual bend when he gets erect.

1 Cover your teeth with your lips. The odd nip here and there is fine, but he doesn't want you to treat his delicate tool like an ear of corn. And don't play rough (unless he asks). Yanking back the foreskin, sucking too hard, pumping up and down like you're trying to draw water from a dry well and snagging any part of it on jewellery (including mouth studs) are all no-nos.

2 Squeeze the shaft of his joystick with one hand to keep him steady and slide your (very) wet mouth over it until your lips meet your hand. That's it. Don't suck – or blow, for that matter. What you (and he) want to start with is a slow up-and-down movement that rubs against the sensitive skin of his penis.

Uncut Version: Don't take him out to play just yet. Instead, moisten the area around the foreskin, then gently edge your tongue under the hood and swirl it around before sliding it down. You can then either hold it down at the base of the shaft or pump it up and down the shaft. BTW, his penis is not a microphone – don't speak into it and ask "how are you doing"! If he is enjoying himself, his moans will give it away.

3 Get your tongue in on the action. Flick it back and forth over the glans or swirl it around its ultra-responsive sides.

Uncut Version: Insert the tip of your tongue underneath his foreskin and swirl it in a circular motion.

4 Get monotonous. Though your mouth may feel as if it's about to fall off, keep steady and keep on suckin'. While lots of variety is good at the beginning, don't change your mouth moves once you get him to the edge or you may have to start all over from scratch.

COME UP FOR AIR
Beginners to fellatio tend to hold their breath. But you don't want to pass out before he does. Here's how to breathe without disrupting the action.

- Whatever his size of tool, you'll be able to take it in your mouth if you exhale before you take the plunge. Here's how it works: When you inhale and then hold your breath, your throat becomes like an inflated balloon, pushing your tongue and the back of your mouth higher. But when you exhale and then hold your breath, the vacuum in your trachea pulls the back of your throat lower, adding up to 5 cm (2 in) to your capacity.

- Try breathing through your nose.

- Work above the blanket (it's at least 40°C/104°F degrees under there with a 50 per cent decrease in oxygen).

Mouth Drills

Try some simple stretching exercises to keep your tongue and sucking muscles limber and strong. Repeat each of the following exercises ten times.

Go Fish: Push your lips all the way forward, rolling the insides out and then opening and closing your mouth much like a guppy.

Spin the Bottle: Tie a string around the neck of a half-filled large bottle of water and lift it using just your lips.

Air Lip: With your mouth firmly closed, push the air upwards so your upper lip blows out. Hold for three seconds, then release.

Tongue Yoga: Stretch your tongue out as far as it will go and try to touch first your nose and then your chin.

Lip Wagger: Circle your tongue around your lips in a clockwise motion and then reverse the motion to counter-clockwise.

Buy a Body Double: Get a double-decker ice-cream cone and slowly lick all around it. Then put the whole mound of ice cream in your mouth. When it starts to drip down the side of the cone, use your tongue to catch the drops.

Sexpert-Approved Tricks To Prevent Mid-Action Injury

- Go "up" on him instead. Kneel on the floor so that his head and shoulders rest on the floor or bed, his back angles towards your stomach and chest, and his bottom rests at your neck level. Then wrap your arms right below his hips to support him. You'll seem strong as a weightlifter, but it's gravity that's doing all the lifting.

- If your jaw gets tired mid-action, switch to licking and kissing his penis and/or stimulating it manually.

- Strategize. Go offside and work him up with some clever hand moves (see pages 70–73). When he's about to score, up the action with some easy oral plays. Run your tongue up and down his shaft to lubricate him, use the tip of your tongue to trace a trail around the base of his penis or gently suck on his balls as you move your hand up and down his shaft. Kiss your way along his member and flick your tongue against the nerve-packed frenulum (the little ridge on the underside where the head meets the shaft). At the last moment, take him fully in your mouth.

- Use a chin rest. Put one pillow beneath his hips and another under your chest. His lower back will be more relaxed, and it'll be easier for him to adjust his knees and legs, allowing for more sensation. Prop your chin on your fist, with your pinkie down, and use a finger to put pressure on his perineum (the magic bit of flesh between his balls and bottom). Watch him hit the roof.

GETTING INTO SHAPE

**Sighs do matter so match your mouth play
to his penis shape and size.**

MONSTER DICK

If he's on the large size, don't be heroic and try to choke up all of
him at once. You'll just end up spitting him right out again. To
stop him from rear-ending your tonsils, have him lie on his back
as you crouch over his crotch. That way you can pull back if he
pushes in too deep. Best of all, you'll leave your hands free so
you can use them on the boys. As he grows to full size, lick the
length of his penis, alternating between sweeping up-and-down
strokes and circular motions. When you're ready to take more
of him into your mouth, try this gag-proof technique: Lick or
lube your hands. Then form a tube with one hand and put it
against your lips. Wrap your mouth around his shaft and slide
your mouth and hand up and down in unison.

Uncut Version: When his appendage is on the XL size, his extra
layer of skin may not retract completely. If you want more of him
to work with, gently push it toward the base of his shaft.

SHORT DICK

If he comes in a mini, make the most of what he's got by taking
the whole thing into your mouth and sucking hard. The tight fit
will make him feel like he's driving a stretch limo.

Uncut Version: Make him feel like the biggest man in the room
by holding one hand in an L position firmly at the base of his
penis, pulling the skin back from the base (in the direction of his

pelvis). Not only does it make him look bigger, but it also heightens sensitivity. You may have to peel back the loose folds of skin to get at his good stuff.

FAT DICK

Yes, it's sweet when you can gobble up his entire sausage. But it isn't really necessary to stuff yourself. Since the most sensitive part of his equipment is in the first 4 cm (1½ in), you can still give him a tongue lashing by concentrating your energies there. Swirl your tongue around the ridge where the head meets the shaft, then gently suck the tip.

Uncut Version: Beware of bunching. You can flatten any lumpy bits with a light push of your hand.

MORE MOUTH MOVES

MINTY MOUTHING

Before tongue diving, swish with a minty mouthwash for 30 seconds. It will make your tongue feel tingly good on their nether regions and make them taste fresh as a stick of gum.

BLOW AND FLICK

Warm him up with this simple move. First, gently take him into your mouth to get him wet from head to base and then dry him off by gently blowing your hot breath over the entire area. Then take the tip of his penis into your mouth, tense your tongue and then make like a snake and flick it with quick darting movements.

Uncut Version: Pull down the foreskin a bit to get to the head.

84

PRICK HIS PRICK

According to acupuncture, there are meridians – interconnected channels of energy – running through the body. To get in touch with his amorous avenue, pop him into your mouth while pressing the base of his big toe with the heel of your hand. Follow-up with a rub along the top of his foot and up the inside of his leg. When you get to his inner thighs, slow down and lighten your pressure to fingertips only while you trace around his testicles and his tummy, ending up on his chest.

PRESSURE POINTS

Sometimes a subtle unexpected pressure makes the difference between a fan-sucking-tastic session and a forgettable one. Here are three jabs he wants you to give him.

- Use your thumbs to press lightly on the sides of his shaft while your tongue does the talking.

- Squish hard against his perineum with your thumb, moving it in tiny circles.

- If you're game and he's down, put your (well-moistened) pointer in his rear (slowly, gently!).

THE TWEAK

Use one hand to guide his penis into your mouth, and then, looking him in the eye, reach up with both hands to tweak his nipples.

Slippery When Wet

Women have (rather handily) built-in lubrication systems, but men don't. So a little extra lube can go a long way towards juicing up your erotic escapade. Here are some handy lube tips.

- Being too generous removes friction (what his penis thrives on). Squeeze one drop on the palm of your hand and one on the tip of his rod and get steamy.

  Uncut Version: You probably won't need much lube since the ultra-sensitive skin is covered by the foreskin.

- If you're working with latex, make sure that the lube you choose is safe (anything containing oil – and that includes chocolate and whipped cream – can make your latex safety net full of holes). Water-based lubes are safe to use with latex; they are sugar-free, nonsticky, and will not stain.

- Make like a wild scientist and sexperiment. Some lubes list glycerine or cinnamon, peppermint or clove oils in the ingredients. When you smear these on his skin and blow, his hotdog will heat up to boiling point. Others contain benzocaine or other mild anaesthetics that numb the skin and trigger an amazing sensation when they wear off. (Heads up: The deadening action means you may also be sucking on his lollipop for a long, long time.) Check out the lube selection at sex shops such as www.blowfish.com and www.annsummers.com.

- Accept no substitutions. Do-it-yourself lubes such as deodorant, hair gel, body lotion and petroleum jelly can cause chemical burns on his most sensitive bits. Follow this rule of thumb: If it's safe to eat, it's probably safe to smear on his dick (honey, ice cream, butter, yogurt, syrup and cheese spread are a few buffet examples – but skip anything spicy like salsa or mustard).

PROPPING HIM UP
Send the amorous action to new heights by adding a few toys to your oral play.

1 Get a buzz on the next time you dive between his legs.

- Use a finger vibrator on his balls, perineum and rear hole.

- Slide a slimline vibrator behind his balls.

- Rest your chin on top of a wand vibrator.

- Hold a small vibrator against your cheek.

2 Want to express your inner erotic artiste? Dip a soft-bristled paintbrush in frosting or chocolate syrup and use his groin as your canvas. Then devour your masterpiece.

3 Wrap a silk scarf or a strand of love beads around your hand and slide it up and down the shaft and head of his penis.

THE SPICE OF LIFE

Variety's always welcome in the land down under (unless it involves sharp objects). The trick lies in knowing how to branch out from your basic slide-lick-suck and work his other bits into the action in a way that is most likely to make him your love slave. Hint: It's all about the build-up. Too much too soon and he could end up losing his concentration while too little too late and you could end up down there until the next millennium. So start small and finish big.

1 Ball Play

- Put both his balls in your mouth at once. Use one hand to circle the top of the sac and gently pull down to bring the balls together into a neat easy-to-swallow package. Then gently suck, hum a little tune and twirl with your tongue.

- As you give his wicket your oral best, reach up and gently pull on his balls, working your hands in tandem with your mouth moves to virtually double the sensation.

- Feverishly flicking your tongue along his raphe (the vertical line in the middle of his scrotal sac) will send an electric volt through his system.

2 Lightly graze your fingernails over his balls and the crease between his thigh and groin. For the first few seconds, barely touch him. As he gets used to the sensation – and his penis starts straightening up – apply more pressure (never scratching!), running the smooth tops of your nails forwards and back. Take care: One misplaced talon could wreak havoc.

3 Give his love warrior a tongue lashing it'll never forget. Plant big wet ones over every inch of him. Start by pressing your tongue against the tip of the glans. Then tap it repeatedly against his frenulum and press it flat against the sides of his hard-on using sweeping strokes as you lick up and down. Do it again... and again. By the third cycle, he'll either be convinced he's died and gone to heaven or he'll have passed out from utter joy.

4 His bottom isn't a black hole to be avoided at all costs. It's actually packed with sensitive nerves just begging for licking. Sweep his backfield with a stiff tongue. If you can't get beyond the bog factor, slip a cut-up condom over the area (the extra material may even boost the sensation). But check out page 226 for washing behind his ears and avoiding infections and STIs before hitting on his back door.

5 Play with his prostate and watch him prostrate himself before you. Hard to reach, this internal walnut-size gland is a pleasure minefield. Wrapping your lips (and hand, if necessary) around the shaft of his penis and, rather than doing your usual up-and-down thing, moving it toward his body will treat him to an inner massage.

TONGUE TWISTERS

Tantalizing tactics that will keep him coming... back for more.

- While moving up his shaft with your mouth, shake your head from side to side (as if you're saying no), letting your tongue follow a corkscrew pattern. Repeat, moving down his shaft.

- Take everything really, really s-l-o-w-l-y.

- Work out – it will help you hold your breath longer.

- Give him a hummer. Simply go "mmmm" for a few seconds on the head of his penis. Work your range: A low pitch makes slow vibrations; a higher one speeds things up.

- Do almost-oral sex where you get real close to his swag and then pass by with just a hot breath. Ignore his pleas. After about five of the longest minutes of his life, gobble him up.

Try this Taoist twist: Go shallow for nine bobs, go deep on the tenth. Then repeat the pattern, but this time do eight shallow bobs and two deep ones. Continue until you've worked your way down to one shallow bob and nine incredibly deep ones. Then do the shimmy, shimmy shake and get into his groove.

DEEP THROATING

Blame the movie, but no man feels his life is complete unless he has been deep-throated at least once. The problem is that the average throat is not made for swallowing a six-to-eight inch (yes, guys – that really is the standard measurement)

sausage whole. To turn her craw into a love passage, she will need to lie back on the bed and hang her head off the edge. He can then stand by the side (on pillows if necessary) so that his penis is lined up with her mouth.

Crank It Up: This is actually a good position for you to practise your gargling skills and swallowing when he shoots. The reason most women gag is because their throat muscles are tight with the expectation of what's to – er – come. But in this position, the throat muscles are too stretched to tense up.

Watch Out: If you feel the urge to gag, take over the action with both hands and come up for air rather than chomping his love stick.

While deep-throating won't necessarily boost his pleasure Q (the most sensitive part of his little friend is the head), it will boost his estimation of your oral powers. Here's how to swallow his sword.

• Pay attention to the angle of his dangle – work from above with an up-curving penis and below with a down-pointing one.

• If you gag easily, point him slightly toward the side of your throat instead of straight down. He won't go in as deep but he'll never notice the difference.

• Stop and relax your throat muscles every 1.5 cm (½ in) or so before letting him go deeper.

• Swallow – when his wand tickles the back your throat, that is. It will help gag your gag reflex and widen things.

ON THE SIDE
Treats you can add to the main menu to make things even more delicious.

- Men are visually stimulated so give him a feast for his eyes by keeping the lights on so he can see his penis move in and out of your mouth.

- Give him a wash 'n' dry. First, blow him with your mouth and then blow him with a hairdryer set on low.

- Do him in a car. If possible, a red convertible. Preferably when he is not driving.

- Apply some bright red lipstick before lipping him off (it double-duties as a great lube).

- Stock up on vitamin C. Make a hole in an orange and place it over the head of his erect member. Gently squeeze and turn the orange and lick up all the oozing juices.

- Take a sip of water, tilting your head backward so it stays in the back of your throat and then take him in your mouth. Ice-cold water will send shivers down his spine while hot (but not scalding) liquid will fire him up.

- Run an ice cube up and down his pole.

BLAST OFF

If his penis swells, his body tenses and his balls draw close to his body, he's gonna blow (shouts of "I'm coooommming" are also a dead give-away). Instantly recall what he does with his body during his intercourse orgasms – does he start jackhammering or does he stay slow and steady? Try mimicking the action with your mouth.

The second his flares go off, up the stimulation by pressing firmly against his perineum.

If you want to bring him around for Round Two when he's already climaxed, caress his ding-dong lightly with your tongue.

THE BIG GULP

Spit or swallow? For most blokes, it's a non-starter. The way they see it, their bodies have been working to produce that brew all day long. It's good stuff. But you may need a few more reasons. Try these on for size.

- Despite appearances, it's only about a teaspoon of semen.

- It's low-calorie and brimming with nutrients.

- The vitamin E content will give your skin a healthy glow.

- Unlike spitting, it's no muss or fuss so you can orally surprise him just about anywhere.

When you sense he's about to come (see Blast Off, page 93), angle him so that his shooting end is pointing at your cheek instead of straight down your throat. To avoid gagging, don't do anything when the gush comes. Just let it sit in your mouth for a moment before swallowing.

THE TASTE TEST
Want to know what his semen will taste like without swallowing a drop? Check his diet.

- Too much fast food or spicy and salty snacks can give him a pungent zest.

- An overindulgence of booze, coffee and ciggies may lead to a bad taste in your mouth.

- Asparagus, broccoli, onions and garlic add a bitter note to his character.

- Bland foods like pasta, fruit and potatoes will keep his taste finger lickin' good.

Heads up: If he used to taste different, he may have an STI such as trichomoniasis or chlamydia. You'll both need to get checked out by a doctor immediately.

A CLEAN FINISH

Ditch the spit kit. There are lots of things you can do with his semen besides swallowing it.

- Give him a dry orgasm. Contrary to popular belief, a man's orgasm and his ejaculation are an inseparable team. A study at the State University of New York Health Science Center at Brooklyn found that men can actually learn to climax three to ten times before ejaculating by flexing their pubococcygeal muscle (the one he uses to control his pee flow).

- Switch to intercourse just before the crucial moment.

- If he catches you off-guard, don't spit back in his face. Instead, let his fluids dribble all over your face.

- Finish him off manually. Make him look forward to it by indulging in his second favourite porn fantasy (after girl-on-girl action) and letting him come all over your chest. Slip him between your breasts and press them together so they massage him as he erupts.

- Don't put your mouth out of action completely. You can still lick the general area while you move over to manhandling him. Make sure you have some tissues or a towel nearby to wipe up the spillage.

SPEED HIM UP

Blowjobs can occasionally be a lot of work (hence the name). If you're at the point where your mind is wandering and wondering whether that cute bag you want to buy went on sale yet, don't throw in the towel.

- Drop everything and zone in on his frenulum. This ultrasensitive area is like a male clitoris – packed with nerve endings, it's a no-fail big-O trigger. With every lick, add a little extra tongue pressure in that one spot until he climaxes.

- Wrap your thumb and index finger around the shaft, about 2.5 cm (1 in) above the base, and pull down while sucking down on the head. He'll probably climax in two minutes tops.

- Launch sequence still not happening? Give it up and make him come another way – with your hand or via intercourse. Save face by sighing, "You made me so hot I can't wait to feel you inside of me."

- If your mouth is tired, stick your tongue out as far as you can and press down. Now you can use your neck muscles instead, and you'll be able to stay the course without getting tongue-tied.

SLOW HIM DOWN

- When you sense that he's reaching his pleasure peak, stop touching him completely for 30 seconds. That should be enough time for him to get in control of himself.

- Take matters into your own hands and firmly press his secret off-spot – the cushy area between the scrotum and the anus – counting one-elephant, two-elephant... until you get to five.

- Try a style that goes on easily (even after he's hardened up) and can be adjusted and taken off, like a Velcro ring (see page 254). The tighter you make it, the more intense the release.

FINALLY, DON'T JUST LIE THERE!

And if you're on the receiving end, getting great oral sex is not the lie-back-and-do-nothing event you think it is. Don't just lie there – do something! Sure, you can hang up the hip action, free your forearms, and save your sweat for the StairMaster. But blissing out and just lying there like you're soaking up the rays is going to make your lover feel a bit like a sex slave. Try using your hands and touching them. Tenderly run your fingers softly over their neck and shoulders, stroke their face, and play with their hair, all of which will make them feel more special and less like something rented for the occasion.

Go ahead and give a performance evaluation. No one feels entirely secure about their oral technique so if they are making you dizzy with delight, tell them how great it feels and that this is the best you've ever felt (leave out the "... in the last 10 minutes" part) and let loose with an occasional "OhmyGodohmy GodohmyGod". If it is not the best you have ever felt in the last 10 minutes, tell them – subtly. Say, "Oh yeah, that feels good, just (insert what you want them to do)" as if to make it a natural next step. If they're hurting you, speak up right away. A simple "Oooh, I'm a little sensitive there" or "Just a bit lighter" can make all the difference.

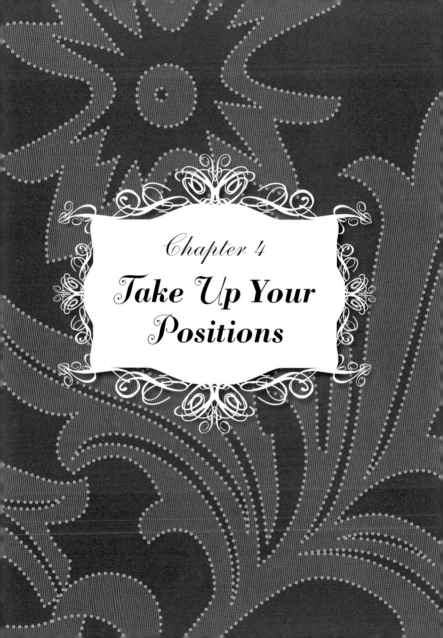

Chapter 4
Take Up Your Positions

TWISTS ON OLDIES BUT GOODIES...
For some Triple X-rated twists on the old in-and-out.

MAN-ON-TOP (AKA "MISSIONARY")

The Old Move: Classic man on top, woman beneath him, face-to-face position. He supports his weight on his arms and you straddle his hips with your legs. It's great for easy thrusting (him) and creating close intimate contact between you.

Make It Better: Do the knee-chest. Raise your legs so that your knees are pressed to your chest then drape your legs over his shoulders. This makes your vagina longer, meaning he can penetrate you more deeply and give you more friction and pressure where you crave it most – your vaginal lips and clitoris.

WOMAN-ON-TOP

The Old Move: Woman-on-top lets you stay in control and show your stuff. Simply sit on his penis and rotate those hips! Sitting is for sex in slow motion; the angles are all wrong for any sort of energetic thrusting. The man sits in a chair or cross-legged on the floor while you sit astride him, usually face-to-face although it can work equally well if you face away from him. This position is good for caressing and intimacy.

Make It Better: Face his toes instead of his head. Then, as you lift yourself up and down, rotate your body in small circles. Tease him by using your vaginal lips to rub his erect penis – tantalize him inch by inch until he's squirming.

STANDING

The Old Move: Standing is best for quickie trysts. But unless you're the same height, it's difficult to manage as he has to hold you up, or you have to stand on a stool so that his penis reaches your vagina.

Make It Better: Turn around and lean over to give him a delicious view of your derriere. Now lift one leg sideways so that he can slip inside you without having to twist. Then close your legs slightly so he doesn't pop out. His hands can slip around to your clitoris to add a little heat.

SIDE-BY-SIDE (AKA "SPOONING")

The Old Move: Side-by-side is a lovely cuddly move that's perfect for canoodling. The classic is spooning (lying on your side facing away from him so that he enters you from behind with his arms wrapped around you).

Make It Better: Both of you lie on your sides, facing the same way. First, you lower your crotch onto his, wrapping your legs around his waist (your arms should be stretched out behind you to support your weight). He encircles your waist with his legs and grips your thighs, then thrusts gently. This way, your partner can tease the turbo-charged nerve endings in the first third of your vagina while tantalizing the packed-with-nerve-endings head of his penis.

REAR-ENTRY (AKA "DOGGIE")

The Old Move: Rear-entry is a pleasure howler, giving ultra-deep penetration. You kneel on all fours and he slips in from behind...

Make It Better: Your partner lies on his back with a pillow beneath his head so he can watch all the action. Facing his feet, you straddle him. Then, placing your hands on the floor first, you back onto his penis. He holds your thighs or bottom tightly while you thrust up and down the entire length of him. This is doing it doggie your way – you have maximum control while your partner gets to savour every sensation without working up too much sweat. It's a fantastic position for an intense G-spot orgasm.

SUPERSIZE YOUR MOVES

Even the most vertically challenged relationship can get stuck in the middle of orgasmic nowhere after awhile. Not to worry. Here are even more twists and variations on popular positions to give bliss to your bods. Many might sound familiar at first, but read closer: each has a special orgasmic spin that'll super-size your pleasure peaks and have you grinning like satisfied frisky fools.

THE MOVE: MISSIONARY

Many women complain that they cannot achieve an orgasm with the man lying on top. These modified version should take things up a notch.

Get Your Leg Over

She lies on her back and puts her legs over her partner's shoulders. He'll have a lot of control over ringing her G-spot bell, and she can play with her clitoris at the same time.

Watch Out: He may get so distracted by watching her navigate her own boat (a favourite among male fantasies) that he forgets to drop anchor in her.

Hit the Hot Spot

He raises his body, resting his weight on his elbows or his outstretched arms. This puts greater pressure on her clitoris. He enters her while she is lying on her back with her legs apart. Once he's inside, she brings her legs close together and has him hook his ankles around her calves and raise himself up slightly on his hands with a small arch in his back. By closing her legs, she will create a more snug entry for him and more continuous clitoral stimulation for her – his groin will be doing a rumba on her hot spot. Also, because it's a short stroke and the angle of his penis in this position will be arching up, he can control his movements better (it's the natural direction of his thrusting) and really reach the front vaginal wall. Meanwhile, she can tighten her lower muscles (her hips, glutes and thighs) to create rhythmic clenching in her pelvic area for an orgasmic blast-off.

Smooth Move: If too much depth in missionary position is making her flinch, he can use shallow strokes so he doesn't come in contact with her cervix.

Watch Out: He'll look a bit like a frog, but this move will make you both feel like royalty.

Switch Legs
This position is going to give him a good workout so he can skip the gym today. He puts his legs outside hers while she keeps hers together. This will bump up the orgasmic rub.

Arch Back
She arches her back a bit so her pelvis is rotated slightly forward to put her clitoris in tickling contact with his penis.

Smooth Move: If arching is too hard to keep up, she can try flexing and unflexing her knees and moving her hips around a lot – although not as precise as back arching, she is bound to get him to hit on her clitoris sooner or later.

THE MOVE: REAR ENTRY

Doing it like the dogs is actually a winner for most couples because of the deep penetration. But it can be better.

She kneels on the floor and lays the upper half of her body across the bed. He comes at her from behind.

Watch Out: Whether he kneels or stands when he comes in for the kill depends on his height.

Control the Depth

She gets into an all fours crawling position and he comes in from behind, either standing or kneeling on the bed behind her. But instead of staying on her hands and knees, she tilts her shoulders downward with her forearms flat on the bed in front of her. The natural curve in her back from this variation will do all the work – expanding or contracting her vaginal wall so she can check how deep he goes. If she arches her back into a small hump, it will shorten her vagina and shift the stimulation down a notch; bend it the other way and she'll get deeper, more intense thrusting action. Plus, he'll get strong yowza's to the head of his penis, the most sensitive part.

Smooth Move: If she doesn't like him to go deep, he should start doing a hula with his hips so his pelvic bones don't push into her derriere.

Watch Out: This pose can make her arms throb after awhile. She can ease off without losing the tingling sensations she is getting in the right places by lying flat on her stomach but arching her bottom upward by placing a pillow under her pelvis. This way, he'll be perfectly positioned to make a direct hit on her G-spot, which is on the front vaginal wall.

Wheelbarrow

Make like a wheelbarrow and roll your way to orgasm – she holds on to the back of a chair and rests her forearms on the seat of the chair while he lifts and supports her legs.

Smooth Move: She can wrap her legs around his waist for additional support.

Watch Out: Make sure you are both strong enough and know exactly what you are doing before even attempting this.

Watch Out For Him: Don't let your weight fall on her, or else you'll be doing it with the blow-up doll in your closet.

No-hands Massage

She gets into her favourite rear pose. Once he is inside of her, she brings her legs together and squeezes slowly and gently. It will be like giving both of your nether regions a no-hands massage.

Watch Out: It's important that she uses a gentle touch or she may end up strangling his penis.

THE MOVE: WOMEN ON TOP

While the old way puts her in control of how fast and hard the action goes, the newer version puts her in charge of how amazing the orgasms will be.

Reverse Action

She faces his toes instead of his head when climbing on top. She then moves in small circles as she lifts herself up and down.

Crank It Up: She can tease him by using her vaginal lips to rub his erect penis, tantalizing him by inches until he's squirming.

Rest on His Shoulders

She places her legs on her partner's shoulders while balancing back on her hands.

Watch Out: He needs to keep his bump and grind to mini size so he doesn't end up knocking her on the floor.

Control the Pleasure

Once she is on top, leaning forward will give her love nub a rubdown, leaning backwards will play bump-the-hot-spot inside her vagina and swaying back and forth will turn her into an orgasmic-drunk

fool. She can also play dominatrix by holding his
arms down while she rides him like he is her own
personal love stud.

Crank It Up: She can try tying him down with a scarf
(loosely or he'll lose circulation in the wrong place).

G-spot Heaven

She straddles him, planting her feet on either side of his hips so
that her breasts are squeezed between her knees. She then starts
rocking her bottom, keeping him in her the whole time. This way,
she can position her body so he's directly hitting her G-spot.

Human Sandwich

He lies on his back, spreading his legs and she lies on top of him,
her legs along his, her feet on his to form a human sandwich.
She controls the pace of lovemaking by dragging herself up and
down against him so that if looked at from above, it would
almost look as if she were swimming over his body.

Smooth Move 1: This is an ideal move for some hot
and heavy smooching.

Smooth Move 2: She's less likely to topple off if he puts his
hands over his head and she holds on to them.

Crank It Up: Closing her legs tight while his remain spread or
him closing his legs or both will send you both on a high-speed
orgasmic ride.

THE MOVE: SIDE-BY-SIDE

The classic way to do this move is fine for those times when you are more in the mood for slow-mo cuddling. The restructured version lets you slip into full orgasmic throttle.

Tense and Relax

You face each other on your sides, super-close together. She raises her upper leg and helps him to slide inside her. She then drapes the leg over his so that it is tight around it. Tensing or relaxing her thighs will help him fit more comfortably inside of her.

Smooth Move: She can brace her feet against the wall to help give her pushing leverage.

Legs Akimbo

She lies on her side, one arm propping up her head. She keeps the bottom leg stretched out and extends the other straight up in the air so that her two legs form an "L". He then straddles her, facing her. He can stay seated or edge his way down so that he is also lying on his side facing her.

Smooth Move: She can rest her top leg along his shoulder.

Crank It Up: She can raise and lower her upper leg to help push him in and out. This will have the added bonus of hitting every sizzle spot between her legs.

THE MOVE: SITTING DOWN

These sit-down variations will make you want to jump up for joy.

Keep Your Legs Shut

This is a sit-down for when the urge strikes you at your desk or even after a romantic meal. He relaxes back against the chair, legs spread comfortable, feet on the floor. She straddles his lap with her back to him, her body inside his legs, her arms stretched out in front of her so they reach the desk/tabletop and her feet suspended in the air. He holds her hips tightly to his lap, thrusting in small circles while she keeps her legs close together. Unlike traditional chair poses, which can be constricting, he'll be able to tease every inch of her vagina with deep up-and-down motions.

Crank It Up: To send her into orgasmic overdrive – he can tilt her forward a bit more and shift gears by using circular strokes.

Take It Kneeling Down

He kneels back so that his bottom is resting on his ankles. She climbs on top facing him – she can squat over him and does the pelvic grind on him.

Crank It Up: She can shimmy up and down until she finds the angle that makes his hammer nail her pleasure nut.

THE MOVE: STANDING
Standing is best for quickie trysts (see pages 143–44). But it usually seems to work better in the movies… until now.

Side Lift
She turns around and leans over to give him a delicious view of her derriere. She then lifts a leg sideways so he can slip inside without having to turn his body like a corkscrew.

Smooth Move: She should close her legs slightly so he doesn't spring out before he's fully cooked.

Crank It Up: His hands can slip around to her front doorbell.

Tongue Laps
She stands with her legs spread wide while he kneels in front of her and practices his tongue laps.

Watch Out: She'll need to have a towel rail, chair – anything she can hold on to for support when her body begins its meltdown.

High Kicks
He stands, holding her high (he can use a wall for leverage) so that she can drape her legs over his arms for support. She holds the back of his neck as he "drops" her up and down.

Watch Out: This is very tiring – he needs to be a gym bunny to pull it off.

Seven Penis Ticklers

**Give his favourite organ a va-va-voom buzz during sex
with these tickler techniques.**

1 While on top, keep his penile skin stretched tight by holding it
down at the base with your fingers. Imagine the heightened
sensitivity you would experience if he stretched the skin around
your exposed clitoris while thrusting against it with his pelvis and
you'll understand why this manoeuvre can send him skyward!

2 Whenever you're on top of him, facing his feet, consider this little
trick: just as he's about to have his orgasm, grasp his toes and pull
gently. It seems that the nerves in his toes are connected to the
ones in his genitals so this extra stimulation increases the intensity
of his ejaculation.

3 When he's lying on top of you during sex, get him to spread
his legs to take the pressure away from his testicles. If too
compressed, they may become under-stimulated.

4 Lie flat on top of him with your legs in between his and squeeze your thighs tightly together. This way, you get to control how deeply he penetrates you and his penis still gets fully massaged.

5 Double his pleasure by turning on his "G-spot". When on top or bottom, reach behind and press on the area between his backside and balls with your forefinger.

6 His penis is never happier than when it's sliding inside you as deep as he possibly can. To give him the ground zero penetration, get into missionary position and lift your legs wide and up. The higher you can go, the further he'll be able to thrust – especially if you push into him with each stroke. (It helps if you wrap your legs around his shoulders.)

7 Sit up straight on top of him – you can face either way to do this. Now grind your pelvis around and around, back and forth. At the same time, squeeze your vaginal muscles tight until you vibrate him into sex heaven.

GET SPICY

Tired of the same old erotic enchilada every night? Mix in some special sauce to heat up your usual sexual menu. Put these on your to-do list tonight and get sizzling.

ROCK AND ROLL

Don't just park yourself in a chair and do it. Rock and roll by turning a straight-back chair into a rocker. He sits first and she climbs on facing him. As your tempo beats up, he slowly tilts her back. When her head is almost on the floor, she opens the angle wide up by putting her feet on his shoulders.

Watch Out: He needs to be able to do two things at once – like holding firmly on to her when he is spontaneously combusting.

THREE WAYS TO RECONNECT

1 Reconnect with each other by sitting in the centre of your bed facing each other. She wraps her legs comfortably around his body so that he is sitting on his thighs (his legs can be splayed straight out or bent at the knees, whichever is more comfortable). She places her right hand at the back of his neck and her left hand at the base of his spine; he mirrors her. When he cranks his shaft in her, he should be giving her love bell a ring-a-ding-ling at the same time. Rock together slowly, rubbing each other's backs, kissing deeply with your eyes open, until you orgasm.

Smooth Move: Put stacks of pillows behind you so either one of you can lean back if the desire to recline hits.

Watch Out: Guys tend to be a little tight and creaky in the muscles. Since the only stiffness this position requires is in his groin area, he should do a few touch-toes stretches to limber up first or he may end up with a muscle spasm, which will cramp your style.

2 Take the above move one step further – he sits on the bed with his legs open wide. She then lies back on the bed, facing him, with her body between his legs. She lifts her ankles up against his shoulders so he can zoom in at a comfy angle.

Smooth Move: The slant will naturally hold her thighs closed, creating a tighter vice-like grip on his dowel.

Crank It Up: She can really put on the squeeze by pumping her PCs (go to pages 32–35 for instant recall) on the outward strokes.

3 Yet a third variation is her lying on her back, again between his legs, but with her legs bent at the knees and pulled back against her until her heels touch her thighs. He sits up close and personal with his battering ram nudging at her castle door. She then places her knees under his armpits. He can then gently pull her closer while he sneaks his way in.

UNCORK HIM

Add some fizz to your play by popping him open like a bottle of champagne. He lies on his back, his legs spread slightly, and his head propped up with a pillow. She "schwings" her legs over his body crosswise and keeps them close together so her legs are positioned making a corner with his. She then sits on top of his thighs or in his lap and leans back on her arms for support. The twist is that she opens her legs slightly as he pops in and begins making slow, swivelling corkscrew motions.

BURN IT BABY

This move is a bit of a workout but the ultimate burn is worth the sweat. He sits with his hands on the ground behind him, his legs splayed open, knees slightly bent. While keeping her hands on the surface for support, she faces him, then straddles his lap, raising her legs so that her right leg rests on his right shoulder and her left leg on his left shoulder. The angle of his dangle will bring on deep, G-spot orgasms.

Smooth Move: Switch the action to the floor, which will give firmer support than a mattress.

Watch Out: Keep your bodies close together so his willy doesn't go flying out unexpectedly.

HIGH FRICTION

Thrusting in and out over and over is something you can do in your sleep. Crank up the action by lying on your sides facing each other. Then lean in and scissor your legs. Hold on close to each other for leverage. This also has the added advantage of creating super close friction. The result: rather than typical in-and-out, you end up grinding in high-orgasmic octane circular motions.

THE BODY TWIST

For those who have done it/seen it and bought the T-shirt, there is the Body Twist. She lies back with her legs up, open and wide apart while he lowers himself on her face-down with his head by her feet and his legs over her hips so that his feet are on either side of her shoulders.

Smooth Move: She can rest her legs on his back and play with his boys while he thrusts backwards.

Crank It Up: For a real joygasmic thrill, she can hold on to his hips and pull herself up in the middle of your love play to give a no-hands massage to your love bits.

TEN HOT, HOT, HOT NEW SEX MOVES

The temperature's rising. To make sure your sex life doesn't go cold, here are ten hot new moves to twist your body into.

1 The angle of this move will turn on its head any feelings you have about typical chick-on-bottom sex. The angle means that her love bump will get plenty of action. She lies on her back. He kneels over her and grabs the headboard. With knees bent, she slowly raises her pelvis until her goods are nose-to-nose with his. Insert and start pounding the bed.

Smooth Move 1: If you're headboard-deprived, he can flatten his palms against the wall instead.

Smooth Move 2: It might help to slip a pillow under her back for support.

2 When you hanker for a quickie but only have access to a tight spot (think car at parent's house), he should assume the squat position on his knees. She lies on her back, resting her knees against her chest and places her feet on his chassis. Start your motors. It's a smooth comfy ride that he can do for quite a few kilometres before running out of gas.

Crank It Up: He can dip and suck her toes.

Watch Out: She should watch the kickback on her orgasms or she may end up landing him one in the chopper.

3 For an ultra-deep move with lots of visual treats for him, try the leg lift. She lies on her side, keeping her bottom leg straight while bending her top leg at the knee. He slides between her legs and, lifts her top leg to rest it on his chest. Now he can enter her.

Smooth Move: He can slip his hand in for some extracurricular activities.

Crank It Up: She starts a fire with the friction by squeezing her PCs (you know the drill – see pages 32–35) tightly as he thrusts.

4 This move mimics the forward bend in yoga, but packs more of an erotic stretch. She bends forward with her legs slightly spread and her arms either hanging loose in front of her (she can rest them on a low chair if she needs the extra balance). He moves in from behind, pulling himself as close to her as possible while holding on to her body for sheer delight.

Crank It Up: Instead of moving in and out, she should grind her behind in circles.

When she wants to feel all of him, she can lie on her stomach with her legs straight and spread slightly. He lies over her, positioning his legs on either side of hers. As he enters her, she should close her legs and cross them at the ankles.

Smooth Move: He can reach under her to play squeeze the melons.

Watch Out: This is a subtle move. Too much thrusting could pop him off her booty mid-action.

5 He lies on his back. She faces him and lowers herself onto his passion crank in a kneeling position. Keeping her knees on the bed, she hooks her feet over the inside of his legs (she can aim for his knees). Grabbing the sheets on either side of his head, she then squeezes her bum, tilts her pelvis upward and moves in small, tight motions. As long as she holds on tight, she can ride him until they both are lassoed by orgasms.

Smooth Move: She should ride his body high so that his pubic bone rubs against her joy button.

6 If her orgasms often play hide-and-seek, you can bring your action into the bathtub. Fill the tub halfway with warm water and keep the water running. She kneels so that she is close to and facing the taps. Leaning forward and holding the walls or sides of the tub for balance will give him room to climb in and play hide the soap from behind. As you grind, she can use her hand to guide the water stream from the tap between her legs (a detachable showerhead comes in handy here).

Crank It Up: He can get in on her pool party by reaching around and washing down her breasts or helping to scrub below her belt.

7 If she is ready for her booty close-up, she can bend over the side of the bed so her stomach and breasts are pressed against the mattress and her feet are on the floor, legs spread comfortably. As he sneaks in from the back, he lifts her legs from just above the knees, holds them apart and thrusts. He gets a full rear end view as well as getting to go in deep and hard. And because nothing in life is free, for all these pleasures, he has to do most of the work.

Crank It Up: By siding in on an upward angle, he will knock, knock, knock against your G-spot's door.

8 She lies facedown across the bed and then squishes her body forward so her head and upper half are hanging off the side. She should put her hands on the floor to hold herself up. He slips between her legs so he is entering her from behind with his legs inside of hers. He can hold on to her for balance so he doesn't go tumbling off the bed.

Smooth Move: Keep it to mini-thrusts that tickle the attention-seeking first few inches of her love boat.

Watch Out: The blood is going to go straight to her head in this position, which can be a pleasure rush for about five minutes. After that, it's a headache. So don't aim for an all-nighter.

9 Make doing push-ups a sheer delight. He lies on the floor face up, lifting his upper body off the floor by pushing up with his backward extended arms. She mounts him in the opposite direction, like she is doing push-ups on his penis (which indeed she will be doing) while facing his feet. She can start pushing. One, two, three...

Crank It Up: If he pushes up with his pelvis, he will manage to simultaneously rub the back wall of her vagina and bliss button.

Watch Out: You may need to take breaks to let the blood rush back into your arms.

10 In this move, everyone's happy – she gets awesome control over the degree of penetration and he worships it because all he has to do is lie there and stare at her bum and then orgasm. What's not to love? To do it, he lies on his back with his knees up. She mounts him with her bottom in his face. After she inserts him, she pumps away, grabbing his knees for support.

Smooth Move: He can sit up slowly while still inside her and give her a great big hug.

TOP TEN KAMA SUTRA POSITIONS

Given the national average of booty moments, even those who do it daily and twice on Sundays would need to invest over a year if they wanted to try every single one of the Kama Sutra positions. Because your days are probably already crunched, here are the ten moves most guaranteed to electrify your play while still giving you time to revel in each other's presence. It's just a simple matter of knowing your "yoni" from your "lingam"! And the winners are…

KEY:

Newbies: These positions don't require much effort but there's no stint on payoff either.

Midwayers: For those who get off on the challenge of mastering these slightly harder poses.

Sexperts: For Kama sexperts only.

Warning: Respect your own flexibility – or lack of it – when striking a new Kama pose or you'll end up in the hospital.

THE PESTLE

She lies with her legs parted wide and held out straight. He slowly enters her "yoni" straight on with his back slightly arched, working up some sparks by pressing his pelvic bone firmly against her love bump and rocking back and forth.

Best For: Newbies

Make It Even Hotter: Slip a pillow under her bottom.

SPLITTING OF THE BAMBOO

He kneels in front of her and she rests one of her legs on his shoulder while leaving the other stretched out. She then alternates this position by switching legs.

Best For: Midwayers

Make It Even Hotter: She can stroke her bliss button while he does his stuff.

PINCERS FROM THE FRONT

He kneels, she sits on his lap with her legs either side of his hips and on the count of one, they both lean back supporting themselves on their hands. He stays absolutely still and she does all the thrusting.

Best For: Newbies

Make It Even Hotter: She lies back and places her legs on his shoulders, holding onto his arms for support. They can then ease into Open Pincer with him clasping her ankles and opening and closing her legs in time to her heave-hos.

THE RIPE MANGO PLUM

She reclines and he kneels on one leg by her side. Grasping her by one leg, he gently pulls it back over her head before inching his way inside.

Best For: Sexperts

Make It Even Hotter: The further he pushes her leg, the more of a head rush she gets as the blood rushes down.

DOOR AJAR

She kneels with one leg on the bed while standing on the other. He does the same behind her and then, holding her standing leg by the ankle, he lifts it up to his waist. She reaches behind and grabs his neck, while he holds her around the waist to keep them balanced.

Best For: Midwayers

Make It Even Hotter: She can reach down and diddle her own pearl deliciously with her free hand.

LIMB TO LIMB

She straddles him and then slowly stretches out so that they are both lined up, limb-to-limb. They hold hands and squeeze together. To help them remain balanced, he keeps his feet flexed so that she can push against them with her toes.

Best For: Newbies

Make It Even Hotter: She raises his arms out to his sides while lifting her upper body, pressing her groin against him even harder – like a snake ready to strike.

TWINING

She lies on her side. He kneels behind her, facing in the direction of her head and slides his knee nearest to her between her legs. She should open her legs just enough to let him in.

Best For: Sexperts

Make It Even Hotter: Once he's in place, she can clamp her legs to work up that tight loving feeling.

CLIMBING THE TREE

So called because it appears as though she is attempting to climb a tree, using his "lingam" as a strong branch to keep her from falling. Start by facing each other, standing. She lifts her leg (right or left, it doesn't matter) and balances it over his shoulder and slips him inside. Kiss, cuddle and run your hands all over each other.

Best For: Sexperts

Make It Even Hotter: With his help, she can lift her other leg so that he completely supports her.

APHRODITE'S DELIGHT

He catches hold of her feet so that her legs form a "circle" and the soles of her feet are pressed against her sides (the higher, the better – the aim is for the soles of her feet to push against her breasts). Clasping her neck, he enters her.

Best For: Midwayers

Make It Even Hotter: She grasps her toes to increase the depth.

WHEEL

He lies flat and she straddles him, lifting one leg and pressing her hands one after the other to slowly rotate around his "lingam" like a wheel.

Best For: Sexperts

Make It Even Hotter: Nibble and kiss each new part of each other's body as it becomes accessible.

HORNIER, HARDER, HOTTER

Even doing the Kama each time you come together can feel as if you're doing the old in-and-out after a while. Knock your knickers off with these scorching spins on the original.

SHAKTI PLUS

In this switcharoo on Shakti (Woman-on-Top), he lies back and arches his back while pointing his property forward. She climbs on, facing her feet, and rear-ends him so that his goods stay bent down (careful he's not so pushed forward that breakage occurs!). The new angle of his dangle allows him to explore every inch of her inner sanctum, especially the oft-ignored sides, providing her with lusty sensations she didn't know existed.

TRANSVERSE PLUS

Sweeten up the classic Side-to-Side with her lying stretched out on one side, one arm holding her head up. She raises her upper leg straight up. Once he hops aboard by straddling her lower leg, she can rest her raised leg on his shoulder. The unique angling gives this move a back-and-forth exhilarating edge over the regular up-and-down, over-and-out routine.

COW PLUS

Transform Cow (Rear Entry) by having her kneel on all fours. He hits home from above, crosswise, as if he's doing a push-up over her body (if he keeps slipping out, he can slide into base from traditional Doggy and swirl sideways). To really rev up the stakes, he leans slightly backwards to take the whole of his weight on one hand and knee. To make her truly sit up and beg, he can move in tiny circular motions with his pelvis.

SHIVA PLUS

For Shiva (Missionary) with a sexy dollop of heat, she lies on her stomach and spreads her legs out slightly. He lies on top of her, and penetrates her from behind, vaginally or anally. She keeps things nice and tight by pressing her legs together (his legs are on the outside of hers). Once you're both comfy, twist around so that you're lying head-to-toe (he may have to turn sideways for a moment to pierce her yoni). Hold on to each other's ankles to stay connected.

FASTER, PUSSYCAT!

Just because the Kama is about otherworldly connections, this doesn't mean you can't get it on quickly when the passion between you becomes fever-pitch. These showstoppers will keep sync mind and body in sync:

1 To get a Rub Down, she lies on her back and lifts her legs so that they're over her ears and parallel to the floor. He kneels in front and, supporting her, presses his upper body against her thighs so that he joins her at the groin. Because her legs are raised, her yoni is narrowed, so there'll be more show-stopping shallow grinding against little-touched nerves than simple head-on deep pounding.

2 She sits on his lap and starts squirming him in to her like a greased pole at a sex club. To get into the beat, she moves and grooves, wriggling her bottom, squeezing her yoni, moving up and down and all around. He can tip her by reaching around and letting his fingers do all the walking over her body, so they're completely connected.

WILD SEX

According to the Kama Sutra, many of the moves we make during sex imitate animals. Get ready to unleash your inner beast (sound effects not included).

CRAB CRAWL

He lies on his back and then lifts himself up in a reverse push-up. She sits on his claw and then rotates to the right, placing her left leg under his right leg. She then brings up her other leg and rests the sole of one foot against his chest, leaning back on her hands. Don't expect to hold this one for more than a minute or two!

GAZELLE AND STALLION

He's kneeling and she wraps her legs around his waist and then, slipping his horn inside, she leans back until her head touches the ground. While she's holding onto his wrists for support and he's lifting her bottom, she raises her bottom up and slings her ankles over his shoulders. With all of the blood rushing to her head and his bone pressing against her G-spot, she will soon sink to the floor in a puddle of glee.

BLOW OF THE BULL
Slip into Shiva (Missionary) but with him leaning out to her right, pulling her knees back up towards her face so that he's resting on the backs of her legs, penetrating her at a deep, deep angle that will make her tingle right down to the tips of her toes.

DOG
He mounts her from behind, gripping her waist. As they bark it up, she twists round to gaze at him.

CAT
She lies on her stomach and he seizes her ankles with one hand, lifting them high while reaching with the other hand to tilt her head back. Purr!

BEE
Any sweet move where she flits her honeytrap around his lingam to make them both buzz.

THE MARE
When she forcibly holds him inside with her pelvic floor muscles and milks him dry.

Chapter 5
Quickies

FOUR REASONS HE WANTS IT NOW
All it takes to plaster a goofy smile on his face is five minutes.

1 Some men… most men… OK… ALL men, at a certain level, have a weakness for rapid sex. It's fast, dirty and has a sense of anonymity about it (according to a University of Vermont study, sex with a stranger is his number-one fantasy).

2 Men are suckers for a little mystery – studies show that the possibility of conquering the unknown is a top reason for why guys stray. Surprising him with some sex-on-the-run will stop him from thinking he knows all your secrets – keeping him as faithful as your neighbourhood St Bernard.

3 Research has found that an occasional quickie can be the answer to a lot of his sexual anxieties. There's no losing sleep over how long he has to last or whether he is giving you enough foreplay. All he has to do is get an erection and use it.

4 Two words: minimal foreplay.

SIX MORE REASONS WHY YOU REALLY SHOULD DO IT NOW…

1 Who has the time or energy for all the prep work that goes into prolonged sex? Dimming the lights to a flattering glow, burning candies, bracing yourself for the never-ending G-spot expedition… yawn. Sex is like dining. Sure, the five-course gourmet deal is delish. But sometimes, nothing but a McDonald's burger will do.

2 While quickies may not be able to save a relationship in nosedive, they're certainly the easiest – and fastest – way to rehab a boring sex life. If you're used to a certain method of making love, a fast body bash can break a ho-hum routine (and it beats dressing up in that French maid's outfit any day).

3 You'll keep the flames burning. Passion doesn't automatically keep going like an Energizer bunny. You've got to work at it, say relationship psychologists. The role of a quickie is to turn up the heat once in a while.

4 Quite simply, your relationship depends on it. According to a study by Ellen Bersheid, PhD, a psychologist who researches close relationships, in order for love to thrive, it's essential that lovers experience minor interruptions so that they can recapture an awareness of their emotional involvement. Because you've behaved unexpectedly and interrupted a pattern (ie, your usual Saturday night making-love-in-bed), he'll be reminded of how much he loves you.

5 Nano-second sex reminds you and him that no matter how crazy life gets, there's always a little space of time to connect as a couple. (Three quickies a week is only 15 minutes. Anyone has time for that.)

6 The after-effects last a long, long time. One poll found that couples who regularly speeded up sex kiss, cuddle and hold hands more. How's that for afterplay?

SIX HURRY-UP HELPS
Tricks to heat the action up in a flash.

1 Get wet. Studies by sex researchers John Wincze, PhD, and Patricia Schriener-Engel, PhD, have shown our body's responses sometimes take time to catch up with our mental urges. Adding a drop of water-based lubricant to the head of the penis before sex (if he wears a glove during sex, add another drop to the tip of the condom) will keep your body and mind on the same sexy page.

2 Forget crooners like Luther Vandross and Natalie Cole. A study from Loyola University discovered that heavy metal and other hard-rock variations get his pulses (and other bits) racing. So make sure you have a Nine Inch Nails or Aerosmith CD in your collection.

3 Stick your schnoz in his underarm. A recent Bern University study found that this is where a whiff of someone's scent can send you into a sexual frenzy. A sniff of lavender and pumpkin pie will have the same stiffening effect on him – the Scent Smell & Taste Treatment and Research Foundation in Chicago discovered that these combined odours increase penile blood-flow by 40 per cent.

4 Carry a quickie kit. Keep condoms, any props like scarves or handcuffs (for a little "lite" bondage), lubrication and a compact mirror and hairbrush (for post-sex sprucing) to hand so in the midst of passion, you don't get stalled on technicalities.

5 Bump up your secret hot spot. Build sexual tension with this indirect pleasure prep: massage the area about one middle finger length below your belly button. Pressing it gently for about three minutes helps promote blood flow, firing up the whole pelvic area.

6 Give him THAT sign.

- Simply take his fingers and put them in your mouth. It will send an instant message to his groin.

- Get right to the point – lift up your shirt and press your cleavage against his back.

- Try blinking in time to his breathing – it's like flashing "SEX" in front of his eyes.

- Place his hands where you want them: on you.

- Create a quickie code, perhaps a wink or a secret handshake, that says in no uncertain terms "You, me, here, now," to preclude any awkward bloopers or long, boring waits in the bathroom for an unwitting partner.

- Stare directly at his crotch.

- When you're out in a public place, disappear for a few minutes then, when you return, hand him your panties.

- Greet him naked.

141

A QUICKIE FIX
**Bed-tested techniques that are guaranteed to make
the Earth move in sync.**

You're Hot, He's Not: The quickest way to get a man hard is to
go straight to the heart of the matter: his penis (a Pirelli calendar
nearby doesn't hurt either). Three tips: use a firm grip, a wet
hand and flick your tongue.

He's Hot, You're Not: You can waste time with him poking here
and prodding there. But no one knows how to warm you up
better than little ol' you. A little spit or lubrication on the finger
will speed things along. Put your hand over his to make him
putty in your hands.

He Needs To Slow Down: According to the Kinsey Institute
clock, a man can go from start to finish in one minute. To pace
himself to last another 120 seconds, he can:

- Flex his PC muscles – when a man contracts his PCs he can
  lower arousal a few notches.

- Breathe deeply – it directs blood away from his penis.

- Open his legs – when he is lying on top, he can spread
  his legs to take pressure off his testicles. When they are
  too compressed, they become over-stimulated.

- Change gears – simply changing positions can halt
  his momentum.

- Take it out – it removes him from the seat of action. Blowing warm air will keep him hot without exciting him to the point of no return.

You Need To Speed Up: Once a woman is hot, she can keep pace with any man. The trick is getting to the race on time.

- Get a head start by beginning without him – give yourself a helping hand.

- Let him help you get a head start with a one minute visit south of the border (studies show oral sex has the double bonus of quickly lubricating and stimulating you in all the right places).

- Position yourself correctly – getting on top will help his penis connect with your clitoris while rear entry is best suited for hands-on sex.

GET IN POSITION
The top moves to master for playing beat-the-clock sex.

STANDING UP

- It can be tricky to match up your love organs if you're different heights so face away from him and bend over so that your hands are flat on the floor and your weight is forward (or just lean against a wall). He simply enters you from behind. Because all you have to do is slip down your knickers (or just wear crotchless), you can take this show on the road – your office desk, the restaurant toilet, wherever the urge strikes.

143

- If he's strong and you're light, try what the Kama Sutra calls Suspended Congress. While he leans back against a wall, you face him, sitting on his joined-together hands (he should lace his fingers), with your arms around his neck. You can move yourself by extending your legs and putting your feet against the wall.

TWO-IN-ONE MOVES

- Anything rear entry gives the deep penetration often needed with quick sex and lets his penis hit the ultrasensitive front of your vaginal wall.

- If you're sitting in a chair, sit away from him as he can then also massage your clitoris. Hooking your leg over the chair leg will create extra friction between your clitoris and his penis.

- Keep your legs together – this straight-laced position can trigger an instant orgasm by making it easier to clench your thigh muscles which actually continue far up enough to stimulate your inner clitoris (the tissue actually extends 9 cm /3½ in – about the length of your middle finger – up into the pelvic area).

- Wear a girdle – sexy – yes! It puts pressure on lower abs which stimulates your inner clitoris (see above). Or get him to use his hand – anything that presses down on the part of your abs just above your pubic mound (his hand, your hand, a stack of bricks) during intercourse should do the trick because it sandwiches your inner clitoris between your tensed muscles and his penis. Extra tip: make sure he's inside of you first as it will be difficult for him to hit the mark otherwise.

THE DOOR JAM

Make use of the entryways to both your body and home (part of the appeal is you may get busted by neighbours). Caution: don't wear socks, it can make things too slippery. Find a narrow doorway. He leans backwards against the door jam while you do the same with the other, straddling him. You can figure out the rest.

THE ONE-MINUTE MOVE

So-called because that's all he'll be able to hold it for unless he's Arnie Schwarzenegger. He sits down on the floor with his legs bent and his feet flat on the floor and his hands on the ground behind him. He pushes his bottom up off the floor, supporting his weight with his arms and legs. You mount, crouching over him, and ride off into the sunset.

JUST DO IT

These six five-second tricks will have you packing thirty minutes of lovemaking into five.

1 Talk dirty. Tell your lover what you want. Explicitly. Some suggestions: "Mmm, squeeze my nipple. Harder. Yes, that feels so good" – and so on. You get the idea. This isn't just to turn him on (though that's definitely a blissful side effect). But according to a *Journal of Sex and Marital Therapy* study, women who can talk freely about sex have a higher degree of sexual satisfaction than those who can't.

2 Go for his jugular. There is evidence that the physiological state of sexual arousal is similar to the physiological stress states of fear, anxiety or threat. In each of these states, blood pressure rises, the pulse quickens, adrenaline is released into the system and the body is energized and alert. Physically, the body is primed, and it may be possible to transform that primed state into a state of sexual excitement.

3 Use your eyes as well as your hands and mouth. A 1986 *Archives of Sexual Behavior* study revealed that both men and women are stimulated by erotic images, so keep the lights on and your eyes wide open.

4 According to one poll, 40 per cent of men questioned are turned gooey by the natural scent of your nether regions. Not surprising since your vagina is a potent source of pheromones, chemicals that attract the opposite sex. Use it to your advantage – touch your vagina and bring the scent to your partners nose.

5 Become a lady in red. The colour crimson is reputed to amp up passion and enthusiasm so wear it when you want some feel-good fire.

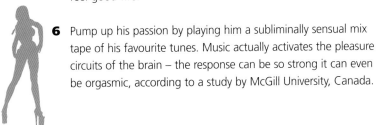

6 Pump up his passion by playing him a subliminally sensual mix tape of his favourite tunes. Music actually activates the pleasure circuits of the brain – the response can be so strong it can even be orgasmic, according to a study by McGill University, Canada.

Speed Busters

You can go from 1,000 to less than zero on the thrillometre in less time than it takes to say, "Ouch". Since you may not have time to restart your play, here's what to avoid in the first place.

- Not kissing first. Avoiding her lips and diving straight for the erogenous zones gives the experience a pay-by-the-hour feeling. Of course, this may be the effect you're going for.

- Breaking contact. The biggest downer about having a quickie is the lack of intimacy. Always keeping in touch with your partner's body makes a big difference. Move your hands together, or stroke them one at a time, in a continual flow. If you have to stop, keep one hand gently resting against your partner's body.

- Giving a wedgie during foreplay. Stroking gently through panties can be very sexy. Pulling the material up between the thighs and yanking it back and forth is not.

- Positioning yourselves incorrectly. The missionary position limits your clitoral stimulation as well as your ability to move around beneath his body. Review previous tips for the most spine (and other bits) tingling moves on the run.

- Getting a non-battery powered vibrator (you don't want to waste precious minutes looking for a convenient outlet).

- Forgetting, in your haste, to use any birth control.

SPIRITUAL QUICKIES

Forget about Tantric celibacy, breathing through alternate
nostrils and all those other new-age fads that are supposed
to achieve nirvana. Face it, what you really want are new
ways to stick his yang in your yin.

TURTLE

Position yourself so you and your man are sitting face to face,
very close together, with his erect penis inside you. Then each link
your elbows under your partner's knees and lift them up to chest
level. In this position you can rock backwards and forwards, and
the motion will have you chanting mantras.

WHEELBARROW

Kneel on the floor with your arms crossed in front of you
(cushioned by a pillow) and your behind in the air. Rest your
head on your crossed arms (or brace your head on the floor itself
if you find that more comfortable). Have your partner stand
behind you and lift your legs up, holding your ankles, until your
lower body is almost at right angles to the floor. Then he should
enter your vagina from the rear. The deep impact will make you
go head over heels.

BACKBEND

Have your lover sit on the bed with his legs extended out in front
of him. Straddle his lap on your knees and lower yourself onto
his erect penis. Then lean into a back bend. (Be careful not to
strain your lower back or his penis – if it hurts either of you, stop
immediately). Rest the top of your head on the bed and reach back

148

with your hands to grasp his feet. Most men think a knee bend is an Olympic feat, so he'll worship you as a sex goddess.

VINE
Start with your lover sitting on a chair. Facing him, lower yourself onto his erect penis until you're sitting on his lap. Wrap your arms and legs tightly around him. Then have him cradle your lower back and buttocks while he slowly stands up.

If he's been hitting the protein powder, he may even be strong enough to lift you up and down on his penis. Otherwise, he can make things easier on himself by propping your back against a wall for support or resting your rear on a table. Enjoy the ride (also a good move for water nymphs).

SWEET LOVE
Lie on your back and pull your knees up to your chest. Your partner clasps your feet in his hands and thrusts from a kneeling position. The deep impact will nudge your G-spot. Variations: for more control, he can grasp your hips; for more pleasure, he can massage your clitoris.

PAIR OF THONGS
Have your partner lean back against a stack of pillows with his legs hanging over the side of the bed. Then kneel astride his hips and lower yourself onto his erect penis. Brace your hands on the pillows behind your partner's head for added leverage and support. He can then reach around and play with whatever sticks out.

UPWARD DOG

Your partner lies flat on his back; you straddle him and lower yourself onto his erect penis. Then slowly stretch out until you're lying straight on top of him, aligned limb to limb. Holding his hands, extend your arms out to the sides and lift your upper body. He keeps his feet flexed so you can push against them with your toes for leverage. Be careful all that body friction doesn't start a fire.

BUFFET

He sits on the floor, his legs spread, with you in his lap facing him and your legs straddling his arms. He then hooks your knees with his elbows and enters you. Thrusting occurs in one of two ways: he can put his hands on your hips and move you or you can lean back on your arms and rock the boat yourself.

HALF MOON

Lie on your side with your upper leg raised. Lying cross-wise to you, your man then inches his body between your open legs – your bodies will now look like an X if seen from above. Once you're joined at the groin, he grabs your shoulders and you anchor on the floor to stabilize each other for a lunar ride.

KNOT

Kneel face to face, then each of you places the same (right or left) and therefore opposite foot flat on the floor and nudges closer, joining genitals. Leaning forward on your planted feet, you rock back and forth for a slow, upright ride to cloud nine.

KNEE-ELBOW

Sexier than it sounds, he leans against a wall or a tree. Stand facing him and lift one leg up, supporting your elbows on his. He can then bend down and lift up your other leg. He should keep his movements shallow or you may both fall over.

SWING

He lies on his back, his legs spread slightly, his head back. Climb on top and literally swing your body forwards and backwards, pumping the two of you to orgasm.

Chapter 6
Scenes & Scenarios

GET OUT OF BED!

Incredibly erotic hot spots for love trysts around the house that will make you leap out of bed.

TABLE ROCKER

You sit on a dresser or table and he stands, facing you. Now edge your bottom down until he can comfortably slip inside you. This body-rocking move angles your vagina just right for a two-in-one G-spot/clit climax.

SOFA STRADDLER

Your partner sits back on a sofa (or comfy chair). As you straddle his lap with your legs splayed apart, your knees bent up against his chest, lean back so you're almost upside-down, with your arms stretched behind you all the way to the floor to support your weight. Thrust back and forth, opening and closing your legs and clamping your PC muscles (see page 32) around him. When you're ready for him to hit his passion peak, squeeze your PC muscles when he's completely inside to send him soaring.

WATER PLAY

He gets in first with his back to one end of the bath, his legs spread out in front of him and his knees slightly bent. (If your bath has taps at one end, make sure this is the way his back is facing.) Now you get in, sitting so you're facing him, with your arms also propping you up from behind. Position your legs so they're bent on either side of his hips and your feet are resting lightly against the edge of the bath (if the bath isn't big enough to get a stable surface, just wrap your legs around his waist). Push your bottom forward, lift your hips a few inches and use one hand to put him inside you.

STAIR STOPPER

Kneel in front of your partner at the landing of a staircase, with both of you facing the stairs. While you reach up and hold on to each side of the staircase for support (or to the stairs themselves), he holds your hips and penetrates you from behind. Be careful not to pull the banisters away!

ON THE WASHING MACHINE

Have him sit on the machine. Now climb up on to his lap, facing away from him (he can keep you in place by encircling you in his arms). Flip on the spin cycle and get ready to vibrate yourselves to a deliciously dirty climax.

GO WILD!

Here's some lurve tools and tips to help keep things sweet between the sheets...

- There's nothing like feathers to tickle his fancy. Have a wide assortment handy – a feather duster, a boa, a quill, a peacock feather. Lie (or tie) him down and lightly brush over his whole love organ area while you sit on top of him. To really make him squirm with delight, concentrate on the spot where his penis meets his balls.

- Put a small scoop of your favourite ice cream flavour in your vagina, lie back and slip him inside you. Alternate with dripping warm (not hot) wax over your bodies (be very careful, you don't want to cause third-degree burns!) to make your blood vessels dance with delight and give him a temperature-raising orgasm. Or try something bubbly like soda or champagne.

- Give him a lap dance. Dress in crotchless panties and have your partner lean back on a strong, comfortable chair. Facing him and with your hands behind you resting on his knees, snuggle onto his lap. Lift your ankles up to rest on his shoulders. Start gyrating by inching yourself back and forth against his erect member. Slip him in and out of you to drive him wild with desire.

- If you have long hair, climb on top of him so you can seductively brush it back and forth across his body during sex.

- Get fruity! A mashed banana or peaches inserted in your vagina is a delightful invitation for him to whoosh his penis around in it. Once you climax, switch to the 69 position for sweet afters.

- Wrap a silk scarf around your hand to stroke him. Rub it all over his body, tying it around his penis or testicles. Then use it to tie his hands or feet together and climb on top of him.

LOCATION, LOCATION, LOCATION
Anywhere, any time, any place...

CONCRETE JUNGLE
Unless you're a masochist, if you're romping on in an alley or road, you'll want minimal ground contact.

- For a hot and raunchy position that stops your clothes from getting dirty and your bum getting cold, he should squat on his heels while you sit on his upper thighs facing him with your weight on your feet. Wrap your arms around him for balance.

- Another no-muss move: Stand facing the wall with your feet about 45 cm (18 in) apart. Standing facing your back with his feet between yours, he bends his knees and enters you from below. Holding your hips to steady himself, he leans back while you lean forward against wall, his hips pressed against yours.

H2-OHHH!
Make your own waves.

- Hold on to your bikini bottoms. You don't want to do the Walk of Shame back to your towel.

- The perfect pool or ocean water level is waist high (any lower and it's embarrassing, any higher and your passion may be swept away). If you're surrounded by sunbathers, hold your breath and sink to the bottom, pull your bikini bottoms to one side and let him perform oral thrill.

- Have him stand up and enter you while you float on your back – now try that when you're landlocked!

- In general, the water temp has to be 15°C (60°F) or above so his erection won't sink. However, the heat in a hot tub can cause blood vessels to dilate so his erection may not be as firm.

- Warning: While the beach seems movie-made for getting swept away, when sand gets in the creases and holds of the vagina, it can cause abrasions (think sandpaper), which makes it easier to catch STDs, including HIV.

- If possible, have him enter you before you get wet and wild so your natural wetness doesn't wash away first.

HOME SWEET HOME
Listen to your mum's advice: Get out of bed!

- The nozzle at your kitchen sink will add new meaning to the phrase, "getting hosed" when used during a quickie.

- Handy for sex in the kitchen or any other confined space is sitting face-to-face and wrapping your legs around his waist and your arms around his neck.

- If you stop on the stairs, stand one step higher to make penetration a snap.

- Straight-back chairs give more room for manoeuvring. You can sit on his lap facing away from him or wrap your legs around him facing him. Or kneel on the chair holding onto the back (though you may topple over if things get vigorous – which we hope they will).

ON THE TOWN
Make a break for it.

- Hit the bathroom when you're at a restaurant. The locked door won't arouse suspicion for at least five minutes (which is all you need). Also, watching yourselves in the mirror as you go at it is pretty damned hot.

- If there's a toilet for the disabled, use it – it has the most leg room. Otherwise go for the ladies as there is more privacy than in the gents.

- If you do it in a dressing room, careful about doing it against shoddy walls (they may collapse). A changing bench or chair is much easier and won't arouse the suspicion of any curious salespeople.

- You can have a quickie without leaving your table at a restaurant if the tablecloth is long. Just use your big toe to masturbate each other.

- At the office, use a chair without wheels and flick on the computer monitor for sexy mood lighting (he sits and you perch on his lap). You can add to the excitement though by logging on to a his-'n'-her site.

- If you're at a boring party, head for a tight closet. He can squat on his knees while you lay on your back resting your knees on your chest and placing your feet on his torso. Start your motors. It's easy to get into and you get lots of deep thrusting.

THE GREAT OUTDOORS
Whatever the scenery, the lack of a ceiling (and the risk of being spotted) will intensify the experience outside.

If you're going to have sex outdoors in any position other than standing, bring a soft blanket with you. Avoid using bug spray and sun block until afterwards – both taste awful!

- Make use of the great outdoors. Sunlight is additive-free Viagra. One theory is that it makes people hornier because it suppresses their melatonin, a hormone believed to be the biological version of a five-course meal (it diminishes sexual desire). At the same time, it's speculated that sunshine amps seratonin and other hormones that makes us more open to back-to-nature nookie.

- Do it in a cucumber patch – according to a study conducted by the Smell & Taste Treatment and Research Foundation, the most arousing smell for women is cucumber (lavender comes in second, great if you're in Provence).

- If passion overtakes you while you're walking in the woods, remember that mozzies love moist dark places – you get the picture (ouch!). Spray yourselves with repellent before heading out. A blanket or sleeping bag will also serve as barrier between you and any creepy crawlies.

- Know what stinging nettles and poison ivy look like (see http://en.wikipedia.org/wiki/Poison_ivy).

- If you want extra wood, choose a tree wider than your hips so it'll hold you up as you lean back against it. If the bark is smooth, you can prop your bum against it and lift your legs so that it supports your weight.

IN AN OUTDOOR RESTAURANT
Ask for the table on the edge. Ensure the tablecloth is long and slide your underwear off. Now sit on his lap side-saddle and get your just desserts!

ON A PARK BENCH
Wear a long, floaty skirt without any knickers and have him wear baggy, easy-access shorts. Keep things on the sly by sitting on his lap crosswise, your thighs at right angles to his. Discreetly lift your skirt so you are butt-naked and wriggle gently until you achieve the desired effect.

A WALL OR TREE IN A PARK
Stand facing the wall or tree with your feet about 45 cm (18 in) apart. He stands behind you, bends his knees (unless you're taller than him) and enters you from below. If he wants to show off, he can hold your hips to steady himself and lean back, while you lean forward against the wall.

ON THE GRASS
Relax on your stomach and elbows, and get your man to lie on top of you with his weight on his arms. Raise your bottom slightly to increase penetration (and avoid ants in your pants!).

IN AN ALLEY, FITTING ROOM OR OTHER NON-LIE-DOWN ZONE

He squats on his heels and you sit, facing him, on his upper thighs with your weight on your feet. Wrap your arms around him for balance. You'd better make this one a quickie!

PLAYGROUND FUN

Give new meaning to the word swinging by making love on a swing. He sits on the chair and she straddles him. To keep her balance, he can either hold her around the waist or gently grip her thighs. To rock and roll, move your bodies back and forth.

More Playground Fun: Another variation of swinging sex is for her to sit on the edge, raise her legs and put them on his shoulders while he stands in front of her. He enters her and grabs the front of the swing. You may have to adjust the height of the swing to get lined up right. He can now move her back and forth with the swing, so that his penis strokes in and out with each movement. Result: a weightless lovemaking sensation.

INTO THE WOODS

The woods are full of thorny pine cones, stinging nettles, fire ants and so much more that's risky to bare bums. Instead of thrashing around on the ground, this yoga-like move keeps all your nakedness and delicate bits away from poking, scratching or burrowing. To get into position, she bends over and touches her knees. He stands with his knees bent and legs shoulder-width apart for balance, and enters her from behind.

Smooth Move: He can hold her hips so that she doesn't tip over and possibly snap his branch. If she keeps toppling over, stand within arm's length of a tree so she can support herself at a 90-degree angle.

Crank It Up: Holding her hips also means he can push deep into her.

Another Tree-hugging Move: Another variation is to repeat the above position with her leaning against the tree, but instead of tilting in the same direction as her, he presses his hips against hers and, holding onto her hips for ballast, leans back in the opposite direction. The opposite pull of your upper bodies makes creates incredible tension – just be sure your friction doesn't heat up into a fire.

ON THE MOVE
Live life in the fast lane.

ON A CAR BONNET (HOOD)
Make sure the engine is cool and car alarm switched off before you drive off! Lie back with your hips at the edge of the bonnet and your legs spread wide. He stands between your legs, lifts them and penetrates you. Pull up to the bumper, baby!

To move the action inside the car, she can sit on his lap facing him with her knees pushed against her chest and her feet on the seat or hooked over the neck rest. You won't be able to get much movement so she should squeeze her thighs to press the horn on their love accessories.

Smooth Move: You can also try it where she is facing away from him with her feet on the car floor.

Join the 60mph club by giving each other a hand-squeezer while driving – the passenger slips their hands between the driver's thighs and explores until their legs involuntarily close with pleasure. This is the signal to pull over and finish the trip (either with more hand signals or one of the moves above).

TAKE A CAB
If you are hailing a taxi, don't worry about the driver when feeding each other's meters – they've seen a lot worse. Fall back into the seat in a passionate embrace. She straddles him and undoes his fly. The overall effect should be a couple of hot and horny holiday makers necking.

Smooth Move: She should slip into a skirt to conceal the action.

Watch Out: Make sure you keep track of the miles so you are not only halfway through by the time you get to your destination.

TUNNEL OF LOVE
If you are tracking it, reserve seats on the train that face each other so you can play groin footsie. When the train hits a tunnel, he can substitute his foot with something more substantial.

WHATEVER FLOATS YOUR BOAT
Doing it in a boat is like making love on a waterbed. But the position you choose isn't as important as how you position yourselves in the boat. Stand close to centre of the boat and

keep your body low. Motorboats and catamarans are the most stable, canoes the least.

Smooth Move: Don't remove personal flotation devices and know how to swim.

Watch Out: If it's a sailboat and it starts keeling (leaning to one side), adjust your side to the opposite side so it rebalances.

WHO SAID BUS JOURNEYS WERE BORING?

Long bus journeys don't have to be a bore. Sit at the back where it's quietest, pretend to take a nap and cuddle up in each other's arms. Using a jacket to hide your groin gropes, pay each other's fare.

Crank It Up: Try to get a seat over the wheel – the bus's vibrations will groove your sexy mood.

JOIN THE MILE HIGH CLUB

When you're flying the friendly skies, get free membership to The Mile High Club (www.milehighclub.com). Wait until you reach cruising altitude to ensure that you are at the required 5,280 feet (1 mile) from the ground.

- If you're in a crowded row, she should dash for a pre-agreed lav as soon as possible. Try to select one that is not visible from the galleys. He waits a minute – but not so long that the service carts are blocking him, then makes his way to the rest room and she lets him in. The attendants will then pass by with the carts, trapping the other passengers in their seats.

All-Purpose Watch Outs:

1 Be ready for turbulence.

2 It is illegal to have sex in an airplane bathroom – so deny it in the unlikely event that you are asked. Tell the flight attendant or other passengers that one of you was ill and the other was playing nurse.

3 To avoid a hard landing, rear entry is best for this cramped spot with her facing the toilet and with one leg up on it.

• If it's a bumpy ride, he should sit on the closed toilet seat and she sits on him facing away from him. This way, neither of you will be to close to the ceiling, risking a concussion.

Smooth Move: Wipe the seat down first.

• If the toilet seat isn't something you want to touch with your bare bottom, she can sit on the edge of the sink with her feet pressed against the opposite wall and door so she keeps from slipping and possibly crash landing on his li'l pilot. He stands between her legs.

Watch Out: Make sure she doesn't toe press the call button.

- If it's a smooth ride, she can stand with her back to him and lean over the sink so he can swoop in from behind. Bonus – you can watch yourselves in the mirror (this beats flying first class every time).

- For mid-air docking in your own seat, first do these moves.

1 Try and get an exit row with lots of legroom.

2 Snag a couple of blankets.

3 Snap off the overhead light.

4 Raise the armrest.

- It's easy to hide a hand job under one of those little airplane blankets. And if you're really sneaky, you can rest your head on your partner's lap and just happen to have oral sex. But try not to let your head bob up and down (unless there's turbulence).

- For full body contact, he can slide his machine into her hangar by having her slide down, shifting sideways so that her back is against the window and her feet are facing towards the aisle. He stretches on top of her and pulls up the blanket to shield the action.

BE A QUICK-CHANGE ARTIST
There's nothing as hot as being yourself – except possibly being yourself being somebody else.

Nurse, Barbie, nun, secretary, schoolgirl, robot, the military, teacher or student, lesbian French maid, housewife – exploring those alter-egos hanging around behind-the-scenes in your erotic fantasies can be a fun and fulfilling way to uncover what turns you on. Remember, you're not going for a Golden Globe here – just great sex.

Role-playing doesn't have to be scary master/slave rape scenes – unless, of course, that's your fantasy. Start off with something simple, like getting a makeover at the cosmetic counter of any department store. It's usually free and the look they come up with is often a cross between teenage slut and middle-aged matron. Or slip into some lacy lingerie that is outside of your usual wardrobe choice. Even if it's not your style, wearing it will make you feel like a different person in bed (read: sexy and empowered). Or pretend to be strangers having anonymous sex.

Other popular skits that can add more spunk to your sex are: doctor and patient ("It's time for your pelvic exam"); road police officer and naughty motorist (handcuffs and a watergun come in handy here); cheerleader and player ("Wanna play with my pom poms?"); headmistress and pupil ("You deserve 40 whacks"); boss and PA ("Your assignment for today…"); and stripper and client (remember to pack some paper money for lap dances).

FANTASY ISLAND
How to make your dreams come true...

Make sharing times easier when it comes to your erotic whimsies. Scribble your top three fantasies on a piece of paper and number them from one to six. Toss a die and pick whichever number comes up with the promise you'll act it out.

Act out an orgy à deux. Close your eyes or use blindfolds and work all your digits and tongues at the same time: play with nipples while using your mouth down below. Slide a dildo in from behind while using a vibe mitt in front. It'll feel like a gangbuster.

If the thought of adding another girl to your love dance makes him liquefy (but not you), arrange to get an at-home rub-down while he watches. You'll get warmed up with a mah-vellous massage and plenty of material to fire your engines later.

GET INTO THE ROLE
Five things to put in your closet right now:

Her	**Him**
Corset	Pirate outfit
Any uniform (nurse, maid)	Any uniform (cop, fireman)
Catsuit (fishnet, latex, silky material)	Leather trousers
Cheerleader	Football player
Boa	Male stripper (think thong)

OSCAR NIGHT

Do it like they do in the movies by re-enacting these steamy love scenes. Best of all, you get the starring role.

SOMETHING WILD

If you don't want to break out the handcuffs, he can use his hands to hold her wrists against the mattress when you are doing it man on top (see page 100).

Crank It Up: He can slide her arms up straight over her head and use one hand to hold both wrists, leaving the other free to roam.

Watch Out: If you do move on to handcuffs, keep track of the key.

9½ WEEKS

Indulge in your own S&M scene but keep it "lite". When doggy–styling, he can give her bottom a light but firm slap with his full hand. Starting out with light smacks will increase the skin's sensitivity without causing pain.

Crank It Up 1: If she requests a repeat engagement, you can use his ties to restrain and a wide, flat spatula to spank.

Crank It Up 2: Move on to the fridge scene for afters.

Watch Out: If he shows up with a full arsenal of S&M toys, she should run for the hills.

THE UNBEARABLE LIGHTNESS OF BEING

Do it with mirrors – place a large one next to the bed. With him on top, she lets her upper body hang off the edge of the mattress, so she can stare at their naked bodies upside down in the mirror.

Smooth Move: She should wear a bowler hat.

Crank It Up: Use a small, soft paintbrush, plush feather or silk scarf to gently stroke your partner's naked body. Don't start with the erogenous zones – work your way there.

SHAKESPEARE IN LOVE

She wraps her naked body in a long, long scarf or sari, which he slowly unrolls while caressing her. Then move on to missionary style (see page100).

Smooth Move: Pick up a long, wide piece of silk from a fabric shop.

Crank It Up: For afterplay, he can write a love sonnet.

TITANIC

Sail the high orgasmic seas in style by getting it on in the back seat of a car. With her on top (see page 100), steam up the windows so no one can see what you're up to.

Watch Out: Avoid crashing into an iceberg by making sure the parking brake is on.

FATAL ATTRACTION
Head for the toilet. He hoists her up and they go at it standing.

Smooth Move: He can balance her by resting her bottom against the sink.

Watch Out 1: If the sink isn't strong, you may both end up crashing to the floor, giving you a sexperience the plumber won't forget in awhile. If it seems like it's creaking against all the extra weight, change direction and use the toilet for balance. Just close the lid first.

Watch Out 2: He should keep her away from his pet bunny.

MORE MOVIE FUN
Try out these starring roles.

1 *Ed Wood*: He dresses in women's clothing

2 *Mrs Robinson*: Young man gets seduced by older woman

3 *The Hunger*: Girl-on-girl vampire sex – bite me!

4 *Street of a Thousand Pleasures*: Sex-slave harems

5 *Secretary*: A feast of mind games, humiliation, bondage and beatings

6 *The Lover*: A young virgin is taught the ropes by older suave lover

7 *Boogie Nights*: Porn star tryouts – 'nuff said

8 *Barbarella*: Sci-fi buffs will get off on the high cult mix of zero-gravity spacesuits and attempted murder by orgasm

9 *Crimes of Passion*: She's a fashion designer by day and a kinky prostitute by night (as if she could be anything else)

10 *Dangerous Liaisons*: Sexy seduction set against the lush costume-drama decadence of 18th-century France

11 *Showgirls*: Dry humping, topless dance audition, numerous strip scenes and pole dances

12 *Caligula*: Manages to pack in rape, incest, bestiality, necrophilia, and sado-masochism – all while wearing togas

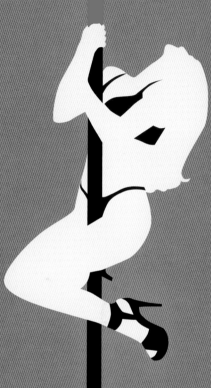

VIRTUAL SEX

Cybersex. Where else can a fat, balding 50-year old bachelor man tell everyone he is really "rugged, powerfully built, tall, broad-shouldered"? Or even "Fifi", a statuesque Las Vegas showgirl? One of the greatest attractions of cybersex is that you can be anyone you want to be, and say anything you want to say.

It's common for cybersexers to assume different personalities, or to invent idealized portraits. Fantasies are, after all, the stuff that cybersex is made of (or perhaps the magnetic rays from monitors are causing men's genitals to mutate to a standard ten-foot size). Cybersex is free, there 24 hours a day, 7 days a week, and it's interactive, with a real person on the other end. Safer than a one-night stand, you don't even have to dress to come to the party.

CYBER RULES

If virtual sex isn't something you do with your lover, then make sure you are alone before logging on. It gets really difficult explaining what you're doing undressing in front of the computer, drooling out of one corner of your mouth, moaning and groaning, while the buzz of various "toys" can be heard.

1 For the same reason, make sure your computer doesn't plant "cookies" or the next person to log on will know exactly where you've been.

2 No matter what you are truly wearing (sweatpants, sweat shirt, torn bathrobe, slippers, T-shirt with stains on the front, knickers that could cover an SUV), always tell your potential cyber partner you are wearing a thong, garter-belt with black stockings, stilettos and a 34DDD bra.

3 When things start steaming, check your spelling before you send that embarrassing typo, ie, "I just love your hot, wet silly", "Oh baby, you have such a big coke", (Hope you got the supersized fries and burger with that.), "Oh fork me hard"!

4 Pay attention to what is going on. Please refrain from asking your cyberpartner to put his "coke" in one place when he had just typed that it was someplace else.

5 Don't fake a cyberorgasm. If the cyber is not going well, let the other person know in the best way you can. Here are some suggestions.

• You suddenly have a burning need to get a manicure (at 3 am).

• Tell him your lover just walked in and you have to log off.

• Weird him out – say you can only orgasm if he'll describe himself taking a dump.

• Say you have to let your dog out.

• Hit him below the belt – type that you are just not feeling this.

Tip: Never give out any personal info online like your full name, where you live, where you work, what your phone number is, credit card numbers and so on. The reason? You don't want people infiltrating your life in case they turn out to be psychos or you get bored. Always sign on with a screen name so you can quickly fade it after the encounter if you want (or need) to.

DIRTY TALKING

Moriaphiliasts (who get aroused by telling dirty jokes) may take it to the extreme, but dirty talk is an easy no-risk way to get risqué. Start with a G-rated vocabulary, then build towards XXX. Instead of murmuring incoherently, get specific, such as "Your mouth feels so warm and wet." Gradually introduce your more graphic thoughts. Get your lover in on the action by asking what they want you to do to them. Even if you know exactly what they want, don't do it until they specifically ask – beg – you to do what they want. You'll soon have them speaking your lingo.

PHONE SEX: SEVEN WAYS TO GET STARTED

There's no need to pay to phone a stranger for this service. Pick up the handset and dial him anytime, anywhere...

Tip: Phone sex can be even better if you misdial!

1 Keep a sexy magazine on hand in case you get dry-mouth.

2 Whisper or talk in a husky voice. What you say matters less than how you say it. "I love scrambled eggs" can sound sexy when spoken in a soft, throaty tone.

3 Play "See Jane Run". In other words, tell him in simple, easy-to-get-quickly sentences exactly what you are doing as you are doing it – "I am playing with my left nipple. It's getting hard. It's making me squirm…" You get the idea. The beauty of phone sex is you can say these things even if you are sitting there in three-day-old jeans doing your nails.

4 Make sure you're speaking the same language. If he says, "pussy" and that makes you steam in a way unintended, or you say "big one-eyed friend" and that makes him giggle, you are not going to get anywhere.

5 Keep talking. If you're finding it hard to form a complete, grammatically correct sentence complete with noun, articles, subject and verb, make a noise – moan, sigh loudly, grunt, throw in a few yeses and pleases. Cry his name. If all else fails, ask him what he wants or how what you are doing makes him feel – it will put the pressure on him to start speaking up.

6 Still tongue-tied? Read a sexy passage from a book.

7 If you still have lockjaw, email or text him.

MAKING A PORNO FLICK

Make pornography part of your romantic routine. Don't just be a passive watcher – use the images as inspiration and try re-enacting the smuttier bits scene by scene. "Is that for me, Big Boy?"

Seeing what you look like in the heat of passion may help you to overcome any fears that your film will end up on YouTube (but of course, that may be part of the excitement). If you're going for an artistic look, go for low lighting. If porn imagery is more your thing, make it light and bright and be sure the sheets look at least a year old. Know one rule before you start: agree that you keep the evidence.

Q Why make your own?

A There won't be:

- (Hopefully) ugly male models with impossibly big dicks and headless women.

- Bogus gurus and ageing sexperts (when was a biology teacher under the duvet erotic?).

- Storylines featuring one woman with gi-normous breasts servicing ten enormous penises.

- Shots of those extremely large penises ejaculating (who thought this was pretty?).

- Shots of semen shooting into women's faces.

- Guys thwacking their wet noodles on women like fly swatters.

Before you start...

1 Get a fake tan so you don't need special lighting to make up for your blinding paleness (and you'll be less conscious about those ten pounds the camera is supposed to add).

2 Get a full body wax.

3 If the above doesn't include your love box, trim your pubic hair.

4 Persuade your man to shave his scrotum (tell him it will make him look bigger if he shaves his ball sack and the hair at the base of his penis).

5 Clear the set of unnecessary objects like tissues, family photographs – anything can distract you when you watch your movie.

6 Use as much warm light as possible (lighting from underneath rather than above).

7 Use high-quality equipment. A good tripod will have a quick-release button so you can whip the camera off and move it quickly when needed.

8 Plan to shoot ten times as much film as you are going to use – you can edit out everything that is unflattering.

9 The position of the camera is important. Mount it on a tripod (high is better for a good overview), look through the viewfinder and mark off the area in which you will be performing so you don't just film the tops of your heads.

10 Turn up the heating – there's nothing less sexy than goose-pimply flesh.

11 Keep at least one item of clothing on – stilettos, a camisole – you'll look better than if you are completely naked.

12 Do some test runs so he gets used to performing in front of the camera (otherwise he may not rise to the occasion).

13 Smear yourself with baby oil to make your skin glisten (but if you're using latex birth control, make it water).

Once the camera's rolling:

1 Vary the shots by moving around as much as possible.

2 Do some gonzo shots (porn-speak for when the person holding the camera shows himself off on film).

3 Don't use the zoom – it never looks good. Move closer if you have to.

4 Exaggerate your sound effects and talk straight to the camera.

5 Use black and white (it's much more flattering).

Tip: Check the camera is actually running – you don't want to find out five hours later as you get ready for replay that you ran out of battery power.

FLATTERING POSITIONS

Bunking Bronco: You sit on top, facing away from him. This way the camera sees your face and boobs bouncing up and down.

Doggy: Position the camera so it's looking up. And remember: if he's directly behind you, the camera will see only his bottom so you need to stick yours in the air.

Oral Sex: His head should be to one side so you can see his tongue darting in and out. He can shoot down when it's his turn (though he might have trouble holding the camera straight).

Chapter 7
Hardcore Fun & Games

POWER GAME RULES

Power games are a part and parcel of any relationship. They only get you in hot water when you regularly play outside of the bedroom. But a little control between the sheets? That's a whole different shebang. As long as your partner is game, these little ploys can give your sex life a kick. And they're a lot quicker and easier to do than most Kama Sutra moves.

Before you start mastering your slipknot, you need to swot up on the rules of the game. Most people think of S&M as no-holds-barred, anything-goes sex play. But getting tied up, whipped, handcuffed, or even mercilessly tickled requires some basic guidelines to keep things safe and sexy. Here's everything you need to know before getting down to business.

Warning: Play safe. Before you begin to trip the light fantastic or book a trip to the wild side of sex, you need to talk with your partner and make sure you are both on the same page. Also know that any type of experimentation is potentially dangerous – yes, that's part of the thrill. But it doesn't mean common sense should fly out the window – these games are more fun when you play safe.

STARTERS' TIPS

- Get yourself in the right frame of mind. Consider this: If you're not ready to talk about your kinky thoughts, you're probably not ready to act on them.

- Start simple. Even if your ultimate fantasy is to create a home dungeon of bondage equipment, start by getting out a few scarves during your next romp and seeing your partner's reaction.

If they seem freaked, they are probably more likely to come around if they think it's their idea. So claim that you were hoping to reenact the Dance of the Seven Veils – but now that they brought it up, it might be fun to try a little tie-up scenario.

- When you're ready to dive deeper, show rather than tell. There is a magazine for every desire under the sun. Try leaving one or two lying around (the bedside table is a good place) and thumb through it with your lover.

- Use the "friend of mine" gambit. This also works when you want to be subtle: "A friend of mine went out with this guy who liked to spank her and she said it was sexy." Along the same lines, use a study: "I read the other day that one out of every ten people has experimented with sadomasochism (true by the way), "that S&M is most popular among educated, middle- and upper-middle-class men and women" (also true), "that getting into kink shows that you're really comfortable with your sexuality and knowing what gets you off" (yup, also true), and that "S&M is like a cardio workout". OK, this last one is a bit of an exaggeration – you will burn more calories when you play rough because doing anything new jumpstarts your adrenalin, which in turn makes your heart pump harder. But how much you work it depends on your fitness level in the first place.

HOW TO TALK THE TALK AND WALK THE WALK
If you don't swot up on the language, you may end up with a boner where you don't want it. Here's a who's who in the S&M world.

Top: This is the person in charge of the games. AKA Dom, Dominant, Master/Mistress.

Bottom: This is the person who gets to lie back and take it. AKA Sub, Submissive, Slave.

Switch: When you like to play both ways.

SM: Sadomasochism – as in "It feels so good when I hurt you/ It feels so good when you hurt me." Insider tip: You call it "S and M" only if you don't do it or if you experiment only occasionally with those handcuffs you keep hidden at the back of the bedside cabinet. If, on the other hand, you own not only handcuffs but also a spanking bench, a flogger, some paraffin wax, an unbreakable Pyrex dildo and various other unmentionables – you call it, simply, SM. S&M is Madonna in kinky outfits. SM is hardcore.

BSDM: Short for Bondage, Discipline, Sadism and Masochism, this is the new politically correct tech term for good old-fashioned SM. Other popular abbreviations include D&S (Dominance and Submission) and B&D (Bondage and Dominance/Discipline). Yabadabadoo!

24/7: Ooh, I need your love, babe – you're into a full-time erotic power exchange 24 hours a day, seven days a week.

SSC: No, not Sizzling, Sexy Cunnilingus – it means Safe, Sane and Consensual.

TPE: Total Power Exchange (think collar, leash and licking boots).

Squick: You've reached your limit and need to say your safe word (make a risk-free jump to xxxx).

TERMS OF AGREEMENT
Before you get down to having hot, kinky sex, you both need to agree on what kind you want to have. Yeah, it takes away some of the thrill of the moment. But so does the shock of having your partner slap a muzzle on you and start commanding you to beg – if that isn't what you had in mind, that is.

- Who is in charge.

- What the scene is. Is spanking OK or just a light tap? Is it OK if you pretend to be a meter maid whipping his sorry butt for parking illegally? Can he visit your back door?

- What your safe word is – these are phrases for telling your lover to either slow down or stop altogether. Think of them as your emergency brakes for when things get too tough, too scary, too painful, too annoying or simply too silly or boring. Plain old "Stop" doesn't work as the other person could interpret it as, "Stop, oh stop, that feels so good, you're the best…" Think of words you normally wouldn't moan between the sheets, such as "Whatev-ah". It's important that when the code word is used, all action stops immediately.

Here's how to apply first aid – no CPR necessary.

- Avoid anything that puts any pressure AT ALL on the front of the neck. It can lead to unconsciousness quickly, as the carotid arteries go right to the brain.

- Never, ever, ever strike the head, neck, lower back (where the kidneys are), chest, backs of knees or abdomen. Continued internal (rather than superficial) pain several hours after a love session may indicate serious damage. Visit the doctor.

- Be careful with gags or very tight laces: Anything that restricts breathing can lead to suffocation – which is obviously not a good thing.

- If a position causes dizziness or nausea, stop and change direction – if you've been sitting, lie down; if you've been lying down, slowly sit up. This can also be a symptom of too-high temperatures, so lower the heat.

MARKS

You can't make an omelette without breaking eggs,
and you can't take part in a heavy-duty pain scene and
not expect to get black and blue. In order of bruising:

• Whipping, surprisingly, seldom causes marks.

• Spanking sometimes does.

• Caning always does, and bondage does more than you'd think.

You can avoid bondage bruises easily by covering the skin first
before you put the ropes around and by taking care when releasing
your partner (pulling rope over the skin may "burn" it). As for
marks caused by hitting, try sticking to well-padded areas like the
bottom, thighs and back if any substantial force is being used.

SIGNS

Cold, blue or white limbs are not an S&M fashion statement. They can be caused by a too-tight rope or a strap, by compressing certain veins or arteries with the weight of the body, or because the hands have been over the head for too long. It's not as scary as it looks (the average arm, leg, hand or foot can do without blood for 45 minutes) but it can be uncomfortable in a not-sexy way. Remove all restraints so the blood flow can resume (a little light massage never hurts at this point). And never leave clamps, rings or weights on for longer than 15 minutes.

WORST-CASE

A jammed bolt is the bad dream of anyone who takes part in a lock-up scene. The main thing is not to panic. Try a few more times. If you're still stuck, don't use a saw. Instead, soap up the skin – you may be able to slip out of your tight spot. Otherwise, you'll need a pair of wire cutters (available from most do-it-yourself stores). For more on how to avoid getting locked-in next time, check out your cuff options on pages 194–95.

Bad Dream Number Two is the possibility of losing something up the bum. Most things will make their own way out given the chance (you could try taking a laxative to ease things along). Avoid this in the future by never inserting anything all the way. And while you're at it, never insert anything that is sharp-edged or breakable and always use plenty of juice. If there's more than a spot of blood and/or pain after anal play, you'll need to get medically checked out.

WAX XXX

The burns from wax drips can feel sizzling sexy – or they can make you scream "Ye-ouch!" To stop wax from getting too hot, always use plain paraffin candles or ones specifically made for dripping on the body (rather than the kind made for creating atmosphere in a room). If the temperature of your play gets too blistering, cool the burned area with cold water (not ice – it will add to the burn) for one minute or more; don't apply petroleum products or any greasy lotions or butter.

HAND SIGNALS

Make sure that you have a safe hand signal if you're using gags (see pages 184 and 188 for more on playing safe). This way, the person being muzzled can still let their partner know if the rope is too tight or the clamps are pinching or they want to stop. Some people hold a hanky – if they drop it, that means stop. Others use a bell, use hand squeezes or raise a pre-agreed finger.

Warning: None of the above should be considered medical advice.

TOYS 'R' LUST

Toys are not a must when it comes to making the scene, but they do make your games more fun. Read on for a few of a kinkster's favourite things – oh, such pretty packages tied up with string!

Remember that bondage equipment is not like a cheap pair of pantyhose – one size fits all. While you can certainly improvise with a handy roll of duct tape and a ball of twine, you may want to work with slightly more erotic materials specifically made for the moment.

Also, cuffs and lubes are must-haves that no self-respecting S&M player would be seen without.

IS LOVE BLIND?

You knew those silk scarves you get from Auntie every year for your birthday were going to come in handy. Tie them with a simple fisherman's knot (see page 206).

Although they come in a variety of materials, leather eye coverings are traditional. Make sure yours has a Velcro backing so you can adjust the size and get in and out easily. Lined blindfolds will be easier on your lids. To really dress the part, opt for one with studs.

Hoods take the blindfold idea one step further. Definitely not for beginners, the feeling of being enclosed can cause instant submission – but it can just as easily cause out-and-out panic. Make the plunge with care.

GAGS

Don't say a word. If you're new to S&M, though, it's wise to avoid gags to start with, so that you can communicate easily with your partner.

Make sure you use breathable material and never use gags when the wearer has a stuffed nose (you figure it out). Also remember to establish a safe hand signal (see above) in case the one being gagged wants to stop play. You can try speciality gags like cock gags (and yes, lads, they do come in different lengths) and ball gags (exactly what it sounds like).

Ball gag: Some find the feeling of being gagged in this way incredibly arousing; others just enjoy the silence it guarantees. Ball gags are not "one size fits all", so your best bet is one made from an easy-fitting jelly-like material. And make sure you agree on a hand signal for when the ball should come out.

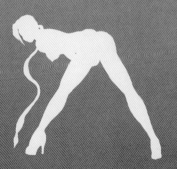

ROPE AND SCARF RESTRAINTS

There are loads of ways to get a grip, so don't hold back.

There are many different lines of rope but the best for newbies is a solid braided nylon or cotton rope. These are strong and, unlike synthetics, won't rub the skin the wrong way; burn the edges of the nylon first so it doesn't fray. They'll also hold knots well and can be easily washed – yes, you should scrub-a-dub-dub your rope. Would you wear your undies again without a wash?

Keep your rope coiled so you can easily use it. It also helps to cut your ropes to specific lengths and mark them so you can quickly find which length you need chop-chop. If you can't remember your scouts training, study the knots on pages 206–7.

Scarves don't actually make great restraints because soft materials tend to tighten under tension – occasionally getting so tight that they need to be cut off. If you must use a scarf, make sure it's not a favourite and keep a pair of scissors nearby in case you get into a tight spot.

CUFFS

Typical cuff materials are leather, rubber and nylon/cotton blends. Unless ultra-pain is your thing, pick up a lined pair so you don't get cuff burns, and be sure to check the fit. It's not enough to check that your cuffs go around your ankle or wrist or testicles – you need to make sure that they're tight enough so you can't slip out, but not so tight you cut off circulation.

Police-style handcuffs seem the obvious choice for booking a bondage scene with your partner in crime, but most end up locking in place or shifting during your fun and games – or you lose the key. Instead, opt for Velcro restraints (which allow quick and easy break-outs), check out faux-fur cuffs that can be colour-coordinated with your outfit, or try cushy leather straps that buckle into place.

STRAPS AND BINDERS

Straps are really just a sexy belt. They come in rubber or nylon but traditionalists use leather. Make sure you get ones that are adjustable. Bondage straps go well with tied-to-the-bed (and to other furniture) scenes. Your strap can double up as a whip.

For arm binders, think long gloves that are pulled over both arms and buckle so that the arms are tied behind the back. They also come in rigid splints. An easier variation on the theme are biceps binders, which just go around the upper arm and across the back, leaving hands free.

If you want something less extreme, try PVC bondage tape. It's reusable and self-sticking so you don't accidentally remove any body hair while under lockdown. This means you don't have to worry about the tape self-tightening as your lover wriggles enticingly on your bed. It also means there won't be any undue pain when you finally remove it. You can use bondage tape to tie wrists, legs or ankles… or you can make like the pros and create some skanky new fetishwear: miniskirts, halter tops, bras and panties are easily made with this stuff. When it's time for removal, you can use scissors or you can peel it off and reuse it again later.

If your bed doesn't have posts, you can still get the spread-eagled look you want by wrapping straps around the legs of the bed. Or try sports sheets (think mattress sheets with a nylon cuff in each corner) – just remember to change your sheets before Grandma pays a visit!

HARNESSES

Like a more elaborate type of strap, harnesses tie around the body. You can get them in traditional leather, chain, rubber and even parachute material for lounging-at-home bondage nights. Some have an open back, with straps down the sides, or a closed back, where the straps cross over. They're usually adjustable to a certain degree, but you should have your measurements to get a better fit. Choose a bra or lower-body harness for a half-trussed look. All styles can come with an attachment for a cock ring or strap-on dildo.

Like edgier his 'n' hers outfits, harnesses come in "top" and "bottom" versions (for your lingo lowdown, see pages 186–87). The "tops" often have straps criss-crossing the chest while the "bottoms" have the chest straps plus extra lengths for a cock ring or to go around the love triangle.

COCK 'N' BULL

Cock and ball harnesses are like cock rings but the strap goes around his meat and two veg. Some have studs and padlocks, but even the most basic kind will help sustain staying power. To get him to snap one on, whisper in his ear that it turns an average wiener into a supersized sausage.

EDGY DRESSING

A collar can be as simple as a necklace or choker, a standard dog collar or a metal, leather, PVC or leather neck band that's been specially made to restrict movement. This last kind usually comes with a metal ring to attach a leash. They may buckle up or fasten with Velcro.

Corsets, in the BSDM world, are designed not to create hourglass curves but to restrict movement. Usually made of latex, PVC or leather, they almost always have lots of laces and zippers to tighten things even more and some rings to keep the wearer tied in place.

These boots were made for walking all over each other. For her, they must be leather or latex, have a spike or stiletto heel, can be lace, zip-up or pull-on, and at least as high as the knee. For him, it's Doc Marten's style all the way.

JOY BUZZERS
Shock yourself with pleasure.

Beat your bedfellow into a quivering heap without laying a finger on them with the OhMiBod Boditalk Escort Vibrator (www.ohmibod.com). A call to your mobile phone triggers this discreet bullet vibrator that stays active for the length of your chat. It elevates phone sex from hokey to hi-tech.

Another take on the absent-but-there theme is the Je Joue (www.jejoue.com), which is controlled remotely via emailed instructions that manoeuvre the textured, circular tip while you're video-chatting.

Get electrified with the Violet Wand (www.violetwand.org), a hand-held generator that comes complete with several glass and metal attachments which, depending on how much power is juiced through them, produce anywhere from a tingling sensation to a full-blown shock to the system.

The Octopus is remote-control fun that no Dom should be without – it's a completely silent, soft silicone cock ring massager.

DILDOS AND BOYS' TOYS

A butt plug is a small cork-shaped toy with a flared end that you shove up the bottom – it can be left in place all day so you never lose that lovin' feeling.

Anal beads are jewels for your bum – they go in then get pulled out again one at a time.

Double-headed dildos are like the pushmi-pullyu – they have a head at each end so there are no fights over sharing. You can get them with the same size heads or one junior and one supersize.

LUBES

For anything anal, silicone-based lubes are slick and slippery-doo-da and stay that way longer. This is because they're not water soluble, and therefore don't get absorbed into the skin. What it all adds up to is fewer applications and no sticky goopiness. Another nice bonus is that silicone lubes don't block pores, so there's less potential for bottom spots. One drawback, though, is that they can be harder to clean up.

For anything involving the mouth, edible lubes will go down better. To smooth your play, check out some of Doc Johnson's Doc's Cocktails (www.docjohnson.com), which come in five mixed-drink flavours.

Get a burn: try warming lubes, which heat up as you rub them on.

Warning: Oil-based lubes (such as massage oil, soap or cooking oils) are to be avoided, as they corrode latex protection and leave behind a coating that can lead to infections.

CANING IT

These tips may help you decide what to use to pack a wallop.

Ticklers are sticks with feathers at the end. A leather tickler is a keep-'em-guessing toy – you can use the soft leather strands to gently tickle your lover's curves – or to deliver a quick sting across their bottom with a tiny flick of the wrist.

A crop is a small (usually leather) whip. Some crops come with a narrow flat "flapper" on one end of a flexible shaft for that oh-so-sexy tickle/whip combo. All you need is a flick of the wrist to power one.

Canes come in a wide variety from the domestic (usually straight and made from bamboo) to the schoolmaster's cane (a curved handle and more traditional). Novice spankers should work with shorter equipment – no longer than 1 m (3 ft) – to hone their accuracy and speed. Thicker canes cut the skin less often but cause more bruising. Thin canes cause more of a stinging feeling than the thud effect of their larger counterparts. It's your choice.

A switch is simply a cane that has been split at the bottom end to produce a fork or two tongues.

Floggers: The word "flogging" may conjure up images of pirates punishing scallywags bound to the mizzenmast – which is one way to get into some scrummy roleplay. Basically, a flogger is any whipping device with a number of leather "tails" or falls tied together to a handle, which is covered with braided leather. There are lots of variations, but the important differences are the type and weight of the leather used for the tails, and how their tips are shaped. Deerskin leather, for example, is very light and soft, making it almost impossible to do much, if any, injury, while bison and bull leather are heavy duty. The most common flogger is the cat-o-nine tails; its nine tails are often braided and end in a plain or knotted tip.

Whips: These are anything with one tail. Real ones can inflict pretty serious damage and are best left to the experts – like bronco busters. If you really want to beat it, try a specially made kind that doesn't hurt no matter how hard it's swung. Some – like one called the "Latex Whip on a Stick" – even sound painful when they come into contact with the skin, but are more likely to make you sigh than cry. Foam rounders or baseball bats also guarantee a soft, satisfying landing.

Spanking paddle: You'll be belting out "Hurts So Good" when your lover gives you a smackdown. There are some scary-looking paddles available (spikes, anyone?) so save your money and use a ping-pong racquet instead. Mix pleasure with the pain by pausing between spankings and massaging their bottom with your hands.

Start out with a small paddle or riding crop, which is easy to guide and more accurate than a flogger or whip. You won't lose your power punch – even lightweight ones can make it uncomfortable for someone to sit down for days.

A slapper has a flat (usually leather) surface with another, hinged flap of leather attached to it so that it makes an extra loud noise upon impact – think sexy sound effects. Some are lined with fleece on the receiving end to cushion the blow. They're small, so you can easily carry one for whenever and wherever the impulse strikes.

PUTTING THE SQUEEZE ON

Clamps are pretty much what they sound like: devices used for gripping onto various body parts such as nipples, balls and vaginal lips. Some nipple clamps are designed to simply give a light nip or a pull. Some are designed to produce a heavy pinch. And some actually have teeth on them that do a biting thing. The crème de la crème are vibrating clamps that give a full-body pinch and buzz. Nipple-to-vulva/penis clamps connect all of your best bits.

A word of advice: Test the clamp on the wrist or less sensitive piece of skin before using it on a sensitive area.

Clips are small devices that grip onto different areas of the body, like BSDM bling for the clitoris, nipples, labia and penis. They usually come in heavy metals like gold and silver, and may be topped with rhinestones and – sigh – mini vibrators.

Cock rings are worn at the base of the penis to keep him going like a Duracell bunny. They come in everything from leather and rubber to nylon and chrome. Some also have vibrators to double both of your pleasure. But don't go on a ring-a-ding marathon – these devices should be worn for no longer than 20 minutes max.

There are many forms of genitorture (the name says it all), but one of the most impressive devices is, without question, the ball crusher. A handsome, heavy chunk of gleaming metal machinery, the base of the ball crusher locks snugly around the testicles, then wing nuts tighten a metal bar securely against them. The testicles are pressed flat – or as flat as they'll go without popping. Picture two rolling pins coming together, mashing the balls. Ouch.

Devious Devices

What to get the serious-minded S&M aficionado.

- In its simplest form, the spanking bench is a wooden sawhorse (with or without a padded top) that the Sub can be bent over to get their just rewards. Some are adjustable, which makes it easier to move onto more intimate play once the spanking is done. High-end benches also come with cuffs and vibrators.

- Assume the position and spreader bars with cuffs will keep your arms and legs spread wide so that your partner has easy access to your entire body.

- Suspension bars are heavy-duty spreader bars that keep you on your toes. You'll need to drill holes in the ceiling to attach it.

- A playground-style sex swing with straps will turn your bedroom into a playground. No, this doesn't mean swinging.

Home Help

You can break the bank – diamond-encrusted snakeskin gag, anyone? – but you don't have to. You probably have enough double-duty items in your home for your own carnal torture kit.

- For restraints, use scarves, neckties, nylons, rope or thick yarn (don't try to undo them afterwards – have scissors nearby).

- Swanky leashes and dog collars can be found at your local pet shop – go for the ones with lots of sparkle.

- While you can always use a scarf for a blindfold, a simple eye mask from a beauty supply shop will stay in place better.

- Flat-headed hairbrushes, slippers or rubber-soled shoes, chopsticks, wooden spoons and rulers will hurt just as good as a specially made paddle.

- Check out your local do-it-yourself store for heavy-duty hardware such as ropes, pulleys, hooks and chains.

- Clothes pegs (clothespins) will do in a pinch for nipple clamps. Wooden ones are a bit kinder than their plastic cousins. Stretch the metal spring in the clothes peg to make it gentler.

- Break out a leather belt as a strap or restraint.

- The best, if ugliest, blindfold/gag/bondage device is probably already stashed somewhere in your bathroom cupboard: an elastic bandage.

- Check out *KinkyCrafts: 99 Do-It-Yourself S/M Toys for the Kinky Handyperson* (edited by Lady Green and Jaymes Easton) for instructions on how to make your own home dungeon with simple household goods.

KNOW THE ROPES

It can be tricky to tie someone up without making it too tight. A good rule of thumb is to tie loosely with lots of turns of the rope. This way, you can easily make things tighter or looser with a simple twist. Make sure that you can easily fit two fingers between the restraint and your partner's skin and they can wiggle their fingers and/or toes. Always keep scissors handy just in case.

Here are three classic knots to put on your belt.

1 Slipknot

This can be easily tied and just as easily untied. Grab anywhere along the length of the rope – this divides the rope into "left" and "right" parts. Twist the rope forming a loop. The direction doesn't matter. Pick up one of the ends. Whichever side you pick up will be the part that slips. Make a fold in the part you picked up. Stick the fold through the loop. Be sure to stick it through in the opposite direction from the one in which the loop went – if the loop had been twisted the other way, you would stick the fold through the loop in the other direction. When you're finished, one part slides and the other doesn't.

2 Fisherman's Knot

An updated version of the basic square knot. Wrap a length of line around the limb and pass one end under all the coils. Notice that the line going under all the coils has to pass over all the coils first. Now cross right over left, then left over right. Pull one "tail". One side of the knot will start to open up while the other side shrinks up. Keep pulling until the expanding side of the knot "swallows" the shrinking side and the knot will flip over on itself.

3 Tying to the bedposts is a bondage classic.
Make a simple round turn around the bedpost. The working end should come over the top of the standing part. Reach under the standing part and hook your finger to the back part of the loop. Pull it straight out away from you. Bring the back loop underneath the standing part. Do not give it any twists or turn it over. Just bring it straight forward. Lift the loop and drop it over the top of the bedpost. The final knot will hold up amazingly well in even the stickiest of ropes. It can withstand pull from variable direction and force. With practice, this knot can be tied using only one hand (untying can be a bit trickier).

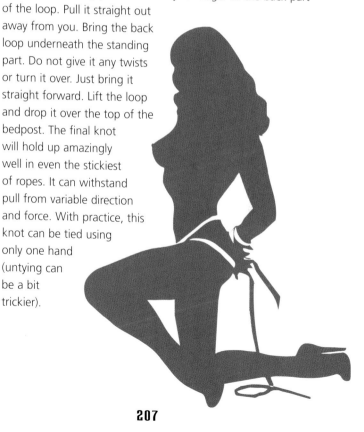

YOUR MISTRESS MANUAL
You get to order him around and have an orgasm...

Greet him dressed in black leather from head-to-toe, stilettos and holding a small paddle or whip. Tell him he has three minutes to get undressed or risk getting punished. Punish him anyway. You choose – you can make him your plaything or order him to ravish you from head to toe.

Practise orgasm control – his. Stroke him but forbid him to climax. Enjoy taking your time with your willing victim – drive him to distraction and bring him to the edge of ecstasy, then back off and make him plead for more!

Up the dominatrix ante – first tell him to do the laundry, cleaning and all of the other household chores. Then, stroke him and forbid him to climax. Want to really make him squirm? Then tie him up and go to town pleasuring yourself. He can't touch until you release him.

NO EQUIPMENT NEEDED
You don't have to own a wardrobe of latex or master more than the basics of the lingo to get into the pain game.

- A simple "Don't move an inch" may be the only restraint you need. Mix in some gentle scratching, pinching and a few light bites and you're playing with power.

- Get things started by lying spread out and telling your lover to do what they will. Then spell out the following scenario: he turns you around, holds your wrists behind your back with one hand, and wraps his other hand around your hair, lightly pulling it while penetrating you, doggy style. After a few minutes, he withdraws, turns you around, places a hand over your neck and goes back in for more.

• Take turns tying each other up spread-eagled and buzzing various pleasure points with a vibrator. Stop and make them beg for more.

• Order him to take off your high-heeled boots and caress your feet. Then tell him to take his hands higher.

• Pros use foot-suspension stirrups to get a hot head-rush, but standing on your head works the same magic. Spread your legs for a little oral action at the same time and the real torture will be seeing how long you can last.

TO LOVE AND OBEY
Sometimes all you want is unadulterated raw sex... with someone else in charge. Here's how to submit instantly – no experience necessary.

• Greet your love master with a deep curtsey that exposes your heaving, corseted breasts, giving him a teaser of what's to come. Guaranteed – he's going to respond with eager-beaver enthusiasm. Or back yourself into a corner and be ready to bolt when your lover closes the door. If he wants you, he'll have to chase you down.

- Find an outfit that makes you feel the role – a particular pair of boots, a certain lipstick colour, a bustier, a French maid's outfit. Get dressed up and ready to play.

- Tell your love tyrant that you've been very, very bad and deserve to be punished. Or try honing his bad-boy persona by encouraging him to sound off and use dirty talk. Tell him you want to be his dirty little girl.

- Encourage him to act as though he's in charge. You need to know that the very sight of you makes him so lust-driven that he can't contain himself. And as his love-thing, you can't refuse. So if he wants to come up behind you while you're washing up and pull down your knickers, there's nothing you can do but lay back and take it.

START A SCENE

Here are eight scenes to get the action started. All of these roles are unisex so you can switch parts. One word of caution: avoid characters and scenarios that are complicated, or that you're not familiar or comfortable with, or you'll spend more time on the prep than the play.

- **Stripper/Customer:** The stripper can touch the client, but the client can't touch the stripper – except to tip.

- **Hooker/Client:** Go high-class or down-and-dirty. Either way, the hooker does all the work.

- **Porn Star/Director:** Pretend to be working with your favourite star, giving them very precise directions on how to please themselves.

- **Older Lover/Inexperienced Partner:** Play an older, experienced lover dominating a shy young playmate, teaching them how to have fun between the sheets.

- **Employee/Boss:** Be the stern boss and teach your employee a lesson in – er – leadership.

- **Patient/Doctor:** Play the medic who gets seduced by their randy patient. Another take is to be a sex therapist unsuccessfully trying to cure a sex fiend.

- **Teacher/Student:** Your pupil has been naughty and needs to be punished.

- **Cop/Thief:** You've been very, very bad and the police are going to have to handcuff you and take you in.

FIT TO BE TIED

Be sure to take your time restraining your lover. Doing it slowly makes the experience more erotic, plus you can make sure you get it right (twist back to pages 206–7 for knotty advice).

That classic bondage position of legs wide open and arms secured got that way mostly because it works. One common mistake is to tie the legs together but that's the wrong kind of torture as he can't gain access.

CHAIR TIE

A chair tie is a great jack-of-all-scenes technique to learn because there's almost always a chair around. Start by tying the ropes over your lover's chest and around to the chair back. Then tie each ankle to a chair leg. If the chair has arms, knot their wrists to them. Otherwise, you can tie their arms behind their back.

LOTUS TIE

Make like a Buddha with the lotus tie. Fold their legs in a floor-sitting position and wrap the ankles together.

CROSSED-LIMBS TIE

Useful when you want to tie your partner's hands at the back or front or to tie the ankles with the knees apart.

First, rest the centre of the rope against their crossed limbs. Coil the rope around the limbs three or four times. Cross the ends of the rope. The one that will go down passes over the one that will go up. This step is needed to change the direction on the rope without pinching or putting undue pressure on the limbs. Then coil a couple of times up and down, passing the rope between the limbs vertically. Finally, finish the binding by tying both ends of the rope with a square knot.

Don't Come Untied: Check that you can pass at least a finger between the ropes and the skin. If you can't, loosen the binding and next time, don't make the coils so tight. It's the looping around the limbs crossways and not the tightness of the ropes that makes the bind secure.

PARALLEL LIMBS TIE

Ties the ankles or wrists so that the arms or knees are pulled tightly together.

First, lay the centre of the rope across your partner's limbs and coil it three or four times around both limbs. When the coils are finished, cross the ropes, the one going down over the one going up. Secure things with a couple of vertical coils and finish with a square knot.

Don't Come Untied: It's the horizontal/vertical hatching that gives this tie its strength so don't pull it too tight while coiling. Make sure you can pass the finger test, slipping one between the rope and the skin.

TIMED AND PRIMED

You don't need to hole up in your bedroom for the weekend to have a bondage blast. These titillating techniques are paced to suit any schedule.

WHEN YOU ONLY HAVE FIVE MINUTES

Use a vibrator. Tie your partner spread-eagled to the bed and rest a vibrator between their legs. While they writhe around trying to get the buzz exactly where they want, you can speed things up even more by adding some oral love.

WHEN YOU HAVE ONLY 15 MINUTES

For his one, he needs to be the bottom. All you need is a plain scarf. Place it around his meat and two veg, and tie in a large square knot, leaving about a foot of fabric on each end to hold on to. As you're riding him, pull on the free ends so that the knot rubs against your clitoris. Constricting his penis and scrotum will lead to a harder erection, which will have you both grinning from ear to ear.

WHEN YOU HAVE 30 MINUTES

Multitask. First, blindfold your partner. Then hit all their passion points at once. When you suck and bite a nipple, use a hand to tease an inner thigh and the other hand to toy with an ear lobe. Remember, they can't see what's coming. Every touch, every action will cause an incredible mix of feelings. Mix and remix every time you do this.

WHEN YOU HAVE AN HOUR

You have two choices:

1 Mess with their mind and mislead where you strike next.
Fasten your partner's hands together and blindfold them for a game of Tease 'n' Tie. Since crawling over them on the bed is pretty much a suspense killer, try to work from the side of the bed. If you can, pull your bed out from the wall. Having 360-degree access means you can do more to them and you have more ability to move around. Also try to minimize how often you lean onto the bed, because, again, they can feel the weight shifting, thus destroying the surprise advantage.

Then drag a finger up their chest, trace it over their lips, and when they think they can suck on it, pop a cherry or hard candy in their mouth – or your tongue. Slowly lick their chest and nipples, then stop for a few seconds. Next, stroke their love triangle. Stop again. Not knowing what you're going to do next really drives them wild, to the point where they'll be begging you to untie them (if they do, make sure they return the favour – and them some).

2 **Play the numbers.**
Once your partner is securely tied and blindfolded, arrange
some toys and implements nearby – clothespegs or clamps,
a vibrator, a paddle or crop, an ice cube, whatever else strikes
your fancy. Assign a number between one and however many
of the various items you have to each one. Then have your
partner in crime pick a number and a part of the body, such
as "seven left nipple", "four inner thigh", or whatever. Use
that implement on that part of the body – clamp a clothespeg
(clothespin) to your partner's left nipple, run the ice cube
along his or her thigh, and so forth. If you have time,
randomly scramble the numbers, and do it again.

WHEN YOU HAVE TWO HOURS
Again, he needs to be the bottom. Tie him to a chair and do a
striptease followed by a lap dance. Grind your groin against his
while rubbing baby oil into your breasts. Lean forward every now
and then and let them hang in his face, just out of tongue reach.

WHEN YOU HAVE ALL NIGHT
Restrain them, stimulate them but don't let them come to
the party fully until you give the OK sign. You can increase his
restraints by securing him in a cock ring, which will also give him
all-night-long staying power (though they should not be worn
for more than 30 minutes at a stretch). You'll need to know
what your partner's point of no return is so that you can stop
all stimulation when they get too close to the edge. When you
do give permission, hold on – the results will be explosive.

GET SENSIBLE
Your senses are the way you experience the world. Putting yours in someone else's control is one of the most submissive things you can do.

BLIND SIGHT

- Cover your lover's eyes. Try to be extra quiet and make them drool with anticipation over when, where and how you touch them next.

  Instead of a blindfold, he should come behind and cover your eyes with his hands. Or you climb on top and cover his eyes while you bounce up and down.

- Blindfold him and give him a lap dance. Up the stakes by tying him to the chair first.

GET IN TOUCH

- Alternate hot and cold sensations by running ice over your lover's body and then dripping hot wax on them. Pay special attention to their moan zones.

- Get clipped: check out pages 203 and 222 for what clips or clamps to use and how.

- There's nothing tinglier for titillating torture than a tickle (say that three times quickly!). Try using a feather or your fingers.

- Lubricate the head of a plunger and press and release it up and down your bodies. It feels like a giant crushing kiss and the extra juice causes a slight suction before release.

- Give each other a full-body massage with some body scrub. Rub as hard as you dare. Or break out loofah mittens and get scratching.

LISTEN UP

- After you blindfold them, keep them even more in the dark with earmuffs to block out sound.

- Get in tune with a torture playlist. At http://fetishexchange.org/scene-music01.shtml, there are music suggestions to groove to for bondage scenes, whipping and flogging. Get down and shake your booty.

MADE TO ODOUR

- The reason leather is big in the S&M world is that it smells oh-so-good. Make him come hither by slipping on a leather glove and playing with yourself. Once your hand is juiced, use it to gag him.

- Add some real spice to your naughty games – crush some whole peppercorns, wrap them in a white handkerchief and secure it with a rubber band. When you feel your man reaching orgasm, have him hold the pepper hanky under your nose just as your climax is on the horizon. The sneeze you'll

have at orgasm will cause your vaginal muscles to clamp
down on him inside you and intensify the orgasmic waves.
Meanwhile, when he has the pepper hanky, the force of his
ejaculation will be intensified as he shoots in tandem with the
force of his sneeze.

WHAT A SPANKER
**Up for some playful paddling? Here are some sizzling ways
to have a spanking good time.**

1 However you sock it to 'em – hand, paddle, hairbrush – start
off striking lightly, then gradually make the beat more intense.
If you hit too strong too soon and too quickly, you will hurt
your lover in a definitely not sexy way.

2 It is the quantity of slaps that does the trick, not so much the
impact and force. Their bottom is not your boss's face, so don't
smash it to a pulp. Start by rubbing it – you can rub one or
both cheeks – and then you should smack only one cheek at
a time. Don't worry, before you know it, they'll turn the
other cheek...

3 The further your hips are bent, the stronger the impact. So it's
better to strike a pose over on your hands and knees, over your
lover's lap, the kitchen table, the bonnet (hood) of your car –
use your imagination. The classic pose lets you brace yourself
against their blows while exposing your rear for a good licking.

4 The key to making your smackdown blissful is location,
location, location. Hit the bull's-eye by aiming where the

butt cheek meets the thigh, or spread the buns and softly spank the anal area with two or three fingers. Spanking close to the genitals will also send the receiver into sweet oblivion.

5 To intensify things, don't hit harder. Instead, relax your wrist. If you're using your hand, alternate between spreading your fingers to widen the stingy effect and cupping your hands to smooth things over. Take a breather after each smack to let the sensation sink in. Mix the moment up with a bottom rub before resuming. For a wildly wanton whack, spank with a leather-gloved hand.

6 Work some light stroking, scratching, and rubbing into your spanking. Don't forget to rub-a-dub-dub their other bits and pieces at the same time to keep things painfully fabulous. If you're using a hairbrush, switch things around and use the bristle side every few smacks.

7 Good spankers have good rhythm. The winning beat is: two light smacks, one slightly harder, then three light smacks and one hard one, and repeat. This build-up will deem you master.

ROLE WITH IT

Spanking and fantasy are the dynamic duo of the S&M scene. Experienced spankers concentrate on the mental foreplay first by announcing the "punishment" and ordering their "badly behaved" partner to stand in the corner and wait for punishment. Favourite plays include daddy or uncle and naughty girl, teacher and badly behaved student, and so on (see also Scenes & Scenarios, pages 154–181). End with a bang – the receiver promises to mend their ways and shows just how good they can be.

I'VE GOT A CRUSH ON YOU

How to put a clamp on your sex play.

1 Don't put the pinch on your lover until they are turned on and always apply it to the tip of their bits. Parts of the body worth pinching are the belly button, inner thigh or arm, vaginal lips, fingers and toes, earlobes and nipples. Try clipping both nipples, then connect them with a chain and gently pull.

2 Remove clips or clamps after 30 minutes to avoid unnecessary pain. The area will still tingle for a few hours, so take advantage of the extra sensitivity by alternating between lightly paddling and tickling the skin.

3 Brush against the clip or clamp or tug at it gently to increase the sensation.

GET WHIPPED INTO SHAPE

If you've ever spanked anyone for a long time, you know that your spanking hand wears out quickly! Well, that's what whips are for. Here's how to give different strokes for different folks.

1 It's all in the aim. First-timers should practise their technique on a pillow. Shoot for a caressing flick rather than a stinging blow.

2 Take it bent over or lying face down. Flogging someone who is standing unsupported can knock them down. Gently drag the striker over the skin, letting the person get a feel for the instrument and excited about what's coming.

3 Time yourself. Go for a strike-rest-strike rhythm of around one stroke every few seconds to give the person on the receiving end time to register the blow and anticipate the next one.

4 Have a few different strikers in your arsenal so that you can play with sensations (see pages 200–2 for the tools). Then you can move from stinging light switches to biting canes, to soft fleeces to a quick tickle and back again.

BALL BUSTERS

His boys are tougher than you think. Here's how to have a balls-up with the family jewels.

1 Give his ball-cock a yank with a light slapping, stiletto prod or even a few flogs. The blood rush will give him an explosive orgasm – but make sure you avoid the underside as you can cause damage to the urethra.

2 Tie his jewels up with leather strips, ribbons or velvet cords. Be as ornamental as you please. Teasing it can be even more artistic, while a few slaps can be extra exciting.

3 Pin the tail on his donkey – you'll be amazed at how many clips and clamps you can get on his penis and balls, especially if he's uncut. He'll love the stinging sensation.

4 Smear some spearmint or peppermint oil over his penis or scrotum for an all-over fresh tingle. Or "paint" melted wax on his brush and peel it off.

5 Catch and release his balls by binding them with a stocking or testicle cuffs and pulling tight before letting go. The tight and loose sensation will have him wriggling on your hook.

6 Make him melt by inserting an ice cube into the end of a condom and then suiting him up.

7 Wrap a silk scarf or stocking around his wood and "shine" it (like you would a shoe). He'll sparkle with pleasure.

WAX PLAY

Full-scale users cover themselves head-to-toe in a polished waxsuit, but all you need are a few melted drops to heat up your homefires.

Play with temperatures. Alternate between hot wax and ice for extremes that will drive your sweetie wild, or use a blindfold.

To get the more sensitive bits of the body like the nipples and family jewels in on the action with all of the pleasure and none of the pain, run your finger along the edge of the candle so you get a wax-covered finger. Then let that finger stroke and poke where it will.

Smear your ride in edible massage wax, and then polish their fenders with your tongue.

HOT WAX TIPS

- Cheap, unscented white candles work better than the perfumed, coloured beeswax kinds because they burn more slowly. Tilt the candle slightly so the hot wax drops one drip at a time.

- If he's a fuzzy wuzzy bear, he should shave first or plan to spend the rest of his life picking wax chunks off his body.

- Oiling the skin before waxing makes removal easier later. Massage oils seem to stay cooler than baby oil, which gets hot under wax.

- Be very careful about lingerie, as some items will melt or burn, sticking to the skin and causing serious burns. Avoid nylon, vinyl, PVC and patent leather.

BOOTY LOVE

The anus is crammed with all sorts of feel-good ultra-sensitive nerve endings. Here's how to get inside. Before any bottom games, play by the rules:

- Groom. Cut and file all your nails. Wash – and not just behind your ears. You may not want to go the whole hog and evacuate the entire area with an enema, but at least make sure things are squeaky clean with warm water and a gentle soap.

- Get kitted out. No matter how clean you get, the bottom is a breeding ground for bacteria. Using latex – either gloves (the kind doctors wear, available at most large chemists), a condom or dental dam – will help prevent infection.

- Juice up. The anus has no natural lubrication, so you'll need to use lots and lots and lots of lube. The crème de la crème are gels made specifically for bottom play. But whichever grease you choose, make sure it's not oil-based (which dissolves latex). Get it all over your hand, the back of your hand, between your fingers. Make a huge mess. And keep applying it as you go. Maintain your site. Never go from anus to mouth, or anus to vagina, without washing carefully (and changing your latex) in between.

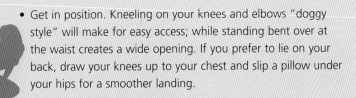

- Get in position. Kneeling on your knees and elbows "doggy style" will make for easy access; while standing bent over at the waist creates a wide opening. If you prefer to lie on your back, draw your knees up to your chest and slip a pillow under your hips for a smoother landing.

1 Tickle his G-spot. The male prostate gland is like an instant orgasm button. To set his off, insert your index finger into his bottom to the second knuckle and press forward, in a firm "come hither" motion. Now gently rub back and forth on the prostate using as much pressure as you can without causing pain. Guarantee – he'll become your love slave forever.

2 Get your whole hand in there. To do this, you don't simply make a fist and ram it home. Work your way in gradually. If they clench, don't pull out. Stay still, let them relax and then continue. When you reach five fingers, you're almost there. Slip your knuckles inside, folding your thumb "inside" your fingers to form a fist. Now the fun begins – rotate and rock your hand in place until you cause an explosion.

Tip: Some people can cause their own big bang by rhythmically contracting and relaxing their sphincter muscles.

3 Kiss ass. Massage, kiss and lick your lover's lower back, thighs, hips and cheeks as you gradually make your way towards their back hole. Widen your tongue to apply pressure over the entire outside area. Suck on the perineum. Now flatten it to push against their opening. Slowly work the tip of your tongue inside and wiggle it around in small circles. Rinse and repeat.

4 Use a small dildo or vibrator to get a back buzz on. Use your hand to work their other bits at the same time.

5 Play "Hide the Sausage". Men love the tight fit of anal sex.

LATEX, LEATHER AND RUBBER – OH MY!

Latex, leather, rubber, vinyl, patent leather, PVC... these are a few of a rubberist's favourite things. It's not just the skintight shiny look – it's the feeling of being enclosed that makes these materials hands-down sexy. Here's how to suit up for every occasion.

- For daily wear, there are cropped shirts, dresses and skirts – all worn as snug and short as possible to show off your curves. Pants are a good option for both sexes as are vests.

- To whip things up, go for something backless to reveal your luscious bottom. Or throw on a pair of leather knickers (crotchless, natch) and matching bra or a bra harness and a G-string or thong. Complete the look with fitted long gloves, stockings (some have lacings) and garters. Guys can slip into crotchless chaps, a G-string leather pouch or leather briefs with a cut-away section for his meat and two veg to peek through.

- If you're into accessories – or just into pain – all of the above also come with studs or rings for bondage and restraint. Slip on a collar and get ready to be led to the land of ecstasy.

- To hell with it – just go all out and slip into a full-body catsuit. Purr-fect. Or try the budget option of paint-on, peel-off liquid latex (www.l8tex.com), which you can use like body paint (you can also paint it over clothing). It comes in a rainbow of colors as well as clear for that shiny enclosed nekkid look. Pour it on and see it dry within minutes (faster if you use a hairdryer).

- Getting in and out. These materials are like a second skin and so getting into them is going to require a certain degree of prep – powder or lube your body before you get dressed. Also, none of this stuff is exactly what you would call "breathable" – so unless you're also into body smells, load up on the deodorant.

- What to do now that you're all suited up? Give him a lap dance. Snuggle onto his lap your hands behind you resting on his knees. Lift your ankles up to rest on his shoulders. Start gyrating by inching your material girl bum back and forth against his erect member. If you have something crotchless on, go ahead and slip him in and out of you to drive him wild with desire.

- Become a looner. Under the premise of: if a latex catsuit is sexy, a latex balloon is sexier – and cheaper – some people enjoy overinflated balloons rubbed against their genitals. Pop!

FETISH FUN

When it comes to sex, there's something weird, wild and wonderful for everyone out there – from tickling torture to dressing head-to-toe in latex. Hey – as long as it's between two (or more) consenting adults, what's the harm in experimenting? Here are some ideas for adding a bit of fetish fun to your sex life.

AIR SUPPLY

Some people get dizzy with pleasure when you cut their air supply. Beginners can try shallow rapid breathing while they play. To bring it up a notch, try gently giving your lover's neck small pulsating squeezes as you lock lips. As their air is cut off, they can feel sensation more intensely. For hardcore asphyxiation aficionados, there are full-head latex hoods, but this is high-risk and can cause death.

ARMPITS

Axillists know that the ultra-thin skin in this area makes it a natural hot spot. Stroke it. Tickle it. Massage it. Lick it. Sniff it. To be a true pit lover, skip the deodorant and shave and get off on each other's natural odour.

BLING AND BODY ART

Make an undercover sexy fashion statement and adorn your body with sparkly nipple charms, clips, shields and earrings, pearl thongs and G-strings, belly jewels, penis and clit bells and clips, belly button clips and rings and back-belly chains. Your friends will wonder what you're smiling about.

Turn your flesh into an erotic work of art with body paints, henna stains or tattoos (temporary or permanent). Try flavoured paints and lick off your masterpieces. Scribble naughty thoughts and sexy sketches. Don't forget to take pictures.

Piercing your nipples, navels, eyebrows, clitoris hoods, penises, labia turn them from mere body parts to 24/7 erotic zones. To make your markings the MVP in your sex games, have your lover lavish them with tongue love. If it's your tongue that's been made into a sex stud, use it like an extra digit, running it over your mate's most sensitive bits.

CHASTITY BELT
It may seem odd to include abstinence in a book on sex, but there is something undeniably hot about enforced chastity. The more you can't have it, the more you want to have it. Now. You can buckle up for a day or for weeks (invest in a higher-end belt which will have toilet-friendly features).

CORSET TRAINING
The corset is to nudity what foreplay is to sex. No other garment is so erotic because none has as loaded an effect on the female form.

A corset will hold you in and boost you up for an amazing streamline appearance. It makes any bust have cleavage to-die-for. Not to mention just slipping into one makes you want to meow like a sex kitten.

Today's corsets come in all sorts of materials from PVC to denim and can be worn under just about anything. But invest in a good fit – the point is to add emphasis to your own sexy curves, not to be restrained (unless that oh-so-tight feeling is part of your love gig). No matter what, your boobs should not be so lifted that you're knocking them with your chin and you shouldn't tighten the laces to the point where you are passing out or your belly is bulging. Once you're in, leave it on to add a wenchy slant to your lovemaking.

DOGGING
Shift your sex play into high gear with a reckless fasten-your-seatbelt-romp in the backseat of a parked car while others watch from the outside. There are dogging websites that post when and where the public showcase will occur. Switch on your interior light when you're ready to start the show. Just be careful not to accidentally release the handbrake.

DOLLS
Guys like to play with dolls too. The queen of synthetic love is the Realdoll (www.realdoll.com) by Abyss Creations. Each Realdoll has a hinged jaw, soft silicone teeth and nipples that "can withstand approximately 400 per cent elongation before tearing". Currently priced at more than £2,500 ($4,000), the dolls are made of solid silicone, just like real porn stars.

ELECTRIC
You can get an extra charge out of sex by clamping your genitals to an electrode and turning up the voltage. Or you can take the safer route and invest in a Violet Wand, a nineteenth-century-style

medical device that stimulates those inner muscles with an electric current. The sensation is like having your lover lightly drag their fingertips over your skin, and then amplifying that feeling by electrifying the touch, so that tiny static sparks erupt from their fingertips. Just don't try it in the bathtub.

If you want to reduce your carbon footprint, you can make your loveplay buzz with erotic electricity by rubbing your feet on a shag carpet while tangoing tongues.

FEED THE KITTY

Is your love life feeling a little vanilla lately? Add flavour to your sexual favours with some munchies. Sausages and unpeeled bananas and cucumbers all double up as delicious dildos.

Run an ice cube up and down and all around and watch him melt. Or let the drips do the work.

Hit your sweet spot and turn your bodies into delicious dessert buffets. Cover each other with gooey gloopy foods like whipped cream, ice cream and chocolate sauce and lick off. In fact, using marshmallow mush, peanut butter and other gooey groceries to make sex tasty is so common, it's got its own name and website: www.splosh.co.uk. There are two types of sploshers: silly slapstick ones who throw cream pies at each other, and sexy, food-as-foreplay *9½ Weeks* devotees. You choose.

Finish up with an Altoid. These curiously strong mints are infamous for boosting mouth sex into the stratosphere, because the peppermint oil gives you that powerful icy-hot feeling. Tuck

a few between your cheek and gum, or crunch them up
completely (to prevent nasty abrasions from cut mints) for
a whole mouthful of that minty goodness. Bon appétit!

GLOVE RUBDOWN

True glove fetishists can get off from wearing a common pair of
pink rubber mitts and washing dishes. But you don't have to do
housework to dip your pinky into this kind of erotic play. Throw
down the gauntlet by slipping into a pair of elbow-length gloves.
Snug and sexy, you can get them in everything from silk to latex.
Some varieties are also fingerless. Work your new digit-wear into
your love scene by giving him a full-body gloved rubdown (take
care how hard you squeeze – silk stains easily!).

HAIRPLAY

Judging from the number of pages catering to hair fascination –
www.hairtostay.com, www.hairydivas.com, www.mylovedhairy.
com (to name just a few of the more tame sites) – hirsute babes
are ultra-hot in certain circles. But plaits, bunches and pigtails are
also making the final cut.

Tip: If it's long lush locks that you're into, climb on top during sex
and seductively brush your tresses back and forth across his body
during sex. After, let him give you a shampoo and rinse.

I SPY

Voyeurism comes from the French word *voir*, meaning "to see".
While secretly spying on someone is a crime, sneaking peeks at
your lover getting off is like a step-by-step of their favourite way
to have sex.

Start up close and personal. Ask them to masturbate in bed while you watch, side by side. Then tell them you want to see them do it again – this time from a distance.

Try having them touch their body in front of the window while you peer in from the outside. They'll get a rush from having their own personal peeper while you feel like you are getting a free peep show.

JAPANESE FETISH

Welcome to Tokyo, the world's most fetish-friendly city. Fetish clubs are on every corner: they've got run-of-the-mill girls in green goo, groin kicking, ear cleaning, nude washing, breast touching, stewardesses… and then there are the local specialties: *ganmen kookegi* (face attack), *nyotaimori* (eating off a naked woman), *unagi* (putting eels in a woman) and *ha daisuki* (a dental exam, where the "porn" features fully clothed women getting their teeth checked).

Also check out *kokigami* – like origami, only sexier. This is the Japanese art of wrapping the penis in a decorative paper costume, such as a dragon or a goose.

SMELL

Don't get sniffy if your lover takes a deep whiff of your undies. The French know the sexy power punch of Pepé le Pew briefs – according to one survey, 40 per cent of Frenchmen and 25 per cent of Frenchwomen do not change their underwear every day.

MUCKY PUPS

If you're into getting down and dirty during sex with oily goo, soapy water or any slimy sloppy stuff that strikes your fancy, welcome to the world of WAM: wet and messy fun (for the ultimate info, click on www.geocities.com/gungesurvey/wamlinks. html). Adding some much needed class, "Wetlook" deals with wet, elegant clothes. At the other end of the spectrum is "Gunge", which covers you in food and pretty much anything but bodily excretions.

To get greasy at home, try covering a flat surface with plastic (a float used for swimming, cheap macs or even garbage bags) and slathering your bodies with oil – you can use common kitchen oil in a pinch, but baby or flavoured heated oils will feel silkier. Take the time to rub each other down, then try to keep your bodies slip sliding against each other as much as possible.

IT'S A WRAP

Proper merinthophiliasts wrap each other up with cling film (plastic wrap), pallet wrap or elastic veterinary wrap. But since novices tend to overlook small details – like breathing holes. A simpler option for the achieving a tight feeling is to roll your lover up tightly in a blanket (preferably made of breathable material).

RUB DOWNS

The French, as usual, have a word for it: *frottage*. It means "rubbing", and when it comes to sex, it's pretty self-explanatory. Frottage is, in its purest form, full-body, face-to-face, crotch-to-crotch contact. It may not be celebrated in videos and porn stories and may not even be talked about too much, but it's a lovely part of making out and can be a full-fledged art in itself. There's not even any technique to learn – just do what feels good and you've got it. Ooh la la!

FOOT AND SHOE FETISHES

There are people out there who will fondle, kiss, orally pleasure and have sex with shoes. They call it "retifism". Women call it shopping. Either way, high-heeled shoes or boots are both seductive and scary at the same time. Nothing can transform a girl into a bona-fide dominatrix faster than slipping on an extra six inches of height. Plus those stiletto spikes can inflict a lot of damage. You'll have him kissing feet in no time. If you want to prolong his agony, give him a peep show with open-toed heels.

Feet are amazingly rich in nerve endings. All your bodily sensations are plugged into the parietal lobe of your brain. It just so happens that genitals and feet share a fence in this sensory neighbourhood. When he's suitably panting, kick off the heels, place your foot firmly on his chest and demand a massage and pedicure. Don't forget to leave a tip.

THREE'S COMPANY

Based on the rationale that if one is fun, two will double the pleasure, the ménage à trios is a hot ticket item in the fetish world. But both men and women tend to fantasize more about inviting an extra babe between the sheets rather than a second Johnny-Come-Lately. It's okay if she brings along a dildo or vibrator to use on him as

a party favour, but women seem to feel more comfortable –
initially, at any rate – getting kinky with another gal pal. The
post-game relationship recovery rate seems to depend on how
much the Number One Girl was made to feel like a third wheel.
If she gets to pick the potential ménage mate and start the
party, she's more likely to feel like a repeat episode.

UPSIDE DOWN
It's true; a rush of blood to the head intensifies orgasm. Pros use
foot-suspension stirrups, but if you don't want to be caught
hanging upside down from the door frame when your granny
pops in unexpectedly, simply have sex sitting facing each other
and lean your head back as things heat up.

VAMPIRES
The extreme version of this fetish is using disposable scalpels and
acupuncture needles to make the red stuff flow. But if this sort of
sex play is not your idea of a bloody good time, restrict yourself
to hickies. Sucking hard on the skin – especially in nerve-sensitive
places like the neck – can be ghoulishly delicious.

Alternatively, go goth. All it takes to transform
yourself into a creature of the night is a black
corset, a black bustle, black nail polish, a heavy
dose of black eye liner, some chain jewellery, a
black leather jacket and a painted-on birthmark in
the shape of a snake. For a real authentic touch,
add white face powder. Enjoy your new-found
menacing air by ordering him to lie still while you
nibble at his neck.

WIGGING OUT

There are burlesque wigs, Goth wigs, heart-shaped wigs, fluorescent wigs, Louis XIV wigs... and those are just for your pubic area. The "merkin" started life in the 1600s as a way for prostitutes to pretty up their honeypot after shaving for vermin. Now it's become a fetishist's dream – decorating the (preshaved) pubic area with a wig of the week. Merkins can be attached with spirit gum or via a transparent G-string.

For a more public change, slip into a head wig. Trying on a different look can make you feel like a different person. And the whole thing gives him the titillating feeling that he's cheating on you, especially if you take on a new badass name – like Bambi or Misty.

WATER SPORTS

This isn't about playing water polo in the nude. Golden showers – either being peed on or peeing on others – tend to be a guy thing. If this is something you're curious about, saying, "Hey honey, I want to piss on you, bend over," is probably not the way to get your bedmate to play. You could ask to see them pee and see how that goes down. (A word of advice: Try diluting the stuff by drinking lots of fruit juice first. It will smell a whole lot sweeter.)

ZZZZZ

Having sex with someone while they're sleeping sounds like assault. But what if they're pretending to be asleep? The person in make-believe dreamland gets the anticipation of wondering where the next kiss or caress is going to be placed on their naked "sleeping" body while the person starting the sex play gets to have total control over everything from foreplay to position.

$\mathcal{S}$extionary

Aeroplane Blonde Someone who has blonde hair on top but still has a black box

Alien An artist with a job

Ambisextrous Someone who is bisexual

Amnesia Sex When you think you are having sex with someone new and you realize you two have done the horizontal mamba before

Anal Assailant A person who prefers anal sex

Anticipointment That low-down feeling you get when an event (such as a romp with a gorgeous man) fails to live up to your expectations

Antiquing Dating someone who is much older than you

Assmosis The process by which that potential Mr Right you met at a party turns into a total ass on your first date

Bachelor Someone who, when forced to choose, will purchase a super-size can of beer over anything comparable in price

Backed Up A glandular condition (with no medical foundation) from which men believe they suffer when they have not had sex for a long time

Bad Breaker-Upper People who tell the truth to end a relationship

Ball Busters Balls that hang so low they get in the way

Bank Account Someone you are going out with just for the free lunch

Before-Play Any misrepresentation of yourself in order to get laid

Below Zero A sex session that leaves you cold

BHI or Boyfriend Hearing Impairment A condition that occurs when a man who never misses the name of the player up to bat, a word his boss says or the amount of money you spent on shoes suddenly goes deaf when you share a horror story about your boss, some gossip about a friend or say it's time to "talk about us".

Bit Flip A sudden 180-degree personality change

Blamestorming Discussing with your boyfriend why some aspect of your relationship isn't working out and who is responsible

Bone of Contention When he has an erection that you did not cause

Born-Again Virgin What you become when you have not had sex for more than six months

Box of Treats Where you keep your vibrator, oil, condoms and lube tube

Boy Friend (as opposed to "boyfriend") A male who has some flaw which makes sleeping with him totally unappealing

Boy Toy Playing with a man who is at least six years your junior

Breakdown Recovery The friends you call after a break-up

Bunny Boiler What you become when a relationship causes you to commit deranged obsessive acts

Buy-sexual "Buy me something, and I'll have sex with you."

Calling in a Substitute Dating someone in order to date his friend

Charitable Orgasm You fake it because he is trying so hard and you feel bad for him

Cheating Paradox It's cheating when the other person does it, not when you do it

Cliterature A selection of one-handed reading material

Code Blue What you call a relationship in trouble

Committing Sexual Perjury Faking it

Computer Man He's hard to figure out and never has enough memory

Contraceptive Dating Avoiding pregnancy by only going out with repulsive men

Crotch Tweaker A guy who can't stop rearranging his family jewels

Data Dump When you divulge your ex-boyfriend's sexual quirks, annoying habits and inner secrets to his new girlfriend

Dating Burnout Suffering one-too-many long boring meals and evenings that either end at your front door or with you skulking out of his apartment at 3 am; you can't be bothered to be charming to any more strangers or even work the room at a party

Dating Down When no one can understand what you could possibly see in the person you are dating since you are obviously so much more attractive/successful/interesting/all three than him/her

Dating White-Out The act of doing-over a huge dating mistake

DBA or Don't Bother Asking What you should do when you spot a man with a child

Deceptionist Someone who pretends to have the same priorities, philosophy, style and enthusiasms as a potential love partner in order to hook him/her

Decoy Someone who fills in between an old relationship and a new one. She/he seems like the Real Thing, but is actually just a distraction until the real Real Thing comes along

Deja Moo When you're out on a first date and you get the feeling you've heard this BS before

Directionally Challenged A lover who heads straight for your candy store without stopping at your main course

Do an RR (Reassess and Repossess) The process by which a dud becomes a stud as soon as you realize someone else wants him too

Double Bed Dread What you get when he is about to move into your space

Double Dipping Dating more than one person at once

Double Whammy When you cheat on your boyfriend with his best friend or he cheats on you with your best friend

Doucher Someone who is obsessed with clean sex

Drag King Women, straight or bi, who dress like men

Drive-By Dumping Ending a relationship without direct confrontation

Earlingus Giving your ear a lick-down

Ego Surfer Someone who constantly fishes for compliments

E-Male A man who is more emotionally open online than he is face-to-face

Er-hem What you call someone when he isn't your boyfriend and isn't your long-term lover (and never will be)

Eurocreep A guy of European descent who has recently come to this country on a short-term work visa. He speaks more than one language, rarely has money, only has models for friends and most certainly has a wife or serious girlfriend back home

Fade Out When someone disappears for a month and then reappears.

Five Pinter Someone you'd only chat up after you've had a few beers

Fixer Upper A guy who needs work but is basically in move-in condition

Flashback Telling your current lover (usually during or just after sex) about your ex – as in, "My ex-lover could last all day and half the night"

Foreign Market Trolling for love outside your usual hunting grounds

Freelancer Someone who is not interested in a long-term relationship of any kind

Free Market What exists when one of you is caught cheating

The Friends Ploy When one of you says, "Can we just be friends?" after sex. What the man is really saying is "Please don't slash my tires" while the woman is really saying "I want to be friends and forget we had sex at all."

Fuck Buddy Someone that you get together with only when you are horny

The Gap Guy His entire wardrobe consists of khakis with a button-down oxford shirt

Glazing Mastering the technique of sleeping with your eyes open (especially useful for when you are on a snooze date)

Goalie When you have sex, he won't stop until you've come

G-Sport Looking for your G-spot

High-Impact Sex High-pressure lovemaking that's hot and hard and comes at high speed

Himbo The male equivalent of a bimbo

Home Bed Advantage That confident feeling you get when having sex in your own environment

IBM or Ideal Breeding Material You can envision making babies with this potential partner

IJA or "I just ate..." Someone who divides the bill to the last penny

IMS or Irritable Male Syndrome His version of PMS

Indecisionitis You can't decide whether to dump him or not

Julia Roberts Rule When on a date, the person who makes a little money pays for the popcorn and movies while the person who makes a lot pays for the champagne and hotel room

Kiss of Death At the end of a date when he kisses you on the nose, chin, cheek, hair – anywhere but your mouth

Late Bloomer A man who takes a long time to become erect but when he does... ooh la la!

Law of Kama Sutra Orgasm There are over 2,000 positions – one of them has to work for you

Law of Relativity How attractive your ex appears to be is directly proportionate to how unattractive your date is

Law of the Jungle An all-purpose appeal-proof statute used by men when they have, in any way, behaved badly

Leftover Sex Sex with your ex

Long Distance Relationship An agonizing experience of triple-digit phone bills, too many DIY orgasms by phone sex and constant suspicion regarding the other person's ability not to cheat (based on your own urges)

Lottery Sex A one in a million chance that you'll have an orgasm

Love At First Sight Disorder What occurs when two extremely horny people meet

Love Terrorist Someone who mindlessly destroys the entire foundations of a relationship in one cruel, death blow

Low-Impact Sex The slow, sweet kind of lovemaking

Maintenance Sex Having sex with someone you've had sex with before but aren't interested in pursuing a long-term relationship with

Male Slut A man good for a quickie – think of him as a shoe that you want to try on but not necessarily buy

M&M Mutual masturbation

Manizer A female with a conquer-all attitude who uses, then loses, men like tissues

Mascara Man He usually runs at the first sign of emotion

Mattressizer Someone who will only have sex in bed

Makeover Queen When you think that with a little effort you can restyle him into the perfect boyfriend

MBD Married But Dating

Mouthing Off Really bad oral sex

Natural Selection The scientific explanation for why there are no good ones left past the age of 35

Navel Lingus The art of making love to the belly button

Necrophiliac Lay When your lover just lies there

Nymphomaniac A man's term for a woman who wants to have sex more often than he does

Out Yourself When you admit that the only type of sex you've ever had has been missionary

Outie A strap-on vibrator

Oversize A larger-than-average stiffy

Part-Time Lesbian A woman who has sex with other women just so she can get the orgasmic benefits

Passing the Sniff Test Having a clean-smelling groin

PDA (Public Displays of Affection) Sex Sex in public

Peer Pressure Sex Sleeping with someone because your friends think he is hot

Petrophobic Someone who is embarrassed to undress in front of a household pet

PG Rating What you give a guy who is probably gay – he is gorgeous, witty, never been in a serious relationship and looks better in your make-up than you

Phonesia The affliction of getting a phone number and then never calling

Pig Pecker Man He comes and then rolls over and plays dead before you're even out of the starting box

Pinocchio Effect Touching your nose when you are telling a lie

Plastic Closet Said about someone who refuses to admit to having cosmetic surgery

The Poppy (Thanksgiving) Effect When your boyfriend breaks up around Remembrance Day or Thanksgiving because it's the pit stop before the Christmas/New Year's romance season

Pre-dating The period of time you spend on the phone and emailing before the actual date takes place

Prophet A sensitive New Age type of guy who will cry over the plight of the whales but is dismissive if you get fired

Puppy A guy with pick-up potential

Relationship Karma An ancient Asian belief where how you treat your boyfriend will determine how you are treated by your next boyfriend

Relationship Résumé Putting a positive spin on your previous partners

Re-Run Accidentally running into a one-night-stand lover

Retro-Dating Going out with a guy you previously dated and nixed because you remember him as a lot better than he really is

Retro-Sex Sex where you do it in a bed in missionary position

Screen Test What you give each other in the early stages of dating to figure out if the relationship is worth pursuing

Secret Single Behaviour The bad habits you indulge when you live by yourself

Se-Men Guys who are obsessed with the speed, amount, consistency, taste and shooting force of their ejaculate

Sexual Camel Someone who can go for a long time between acts of sex

Short Run The length of time one must keep up a relationship after sex (generally two weeks)

Shrinkage His penis experiences this when dipped in cold water

Sixty-Eighter One of you gives the other oral sex with the understanding that the one receiving "owes" the giver

Size Queen A guy who is obsessed with his penis statistics and hopes he qualifies for an oversize

Soregasm What you get when he wants to do it and you don't

Soul Mate A man you dumped who is now going out with another woman

Speed Shooter Someone who ejaculates in 60 seconds or less

Spill Master Someone who takes control of their own fluids

Step-Ins What you use to get off when he isn't doing it for you

Swiped Out What you are when the guy you are with never has any money, sending you on endless trips to get cash

Terror Sex No-contraception sex

Therapeutically Correct Someone who refuses to speak in anything other than the first person and who begins and ends every sentence with what he wants, needs or dislikes, without any room for you to express your desires

Three-ply Someone into threesomes

The Toad Defence What you make after spending money, time and energy to get better acquainted with a person whom you don't especially like in the hope that you will be more attracted to him in the future

Tongue-whipped He's a loser but he gives great oral sex

Trampage What you go on when you sleep with more than one man in a week

Trendoid Well-dressed and confident, his wardrobe will make yours look pathetic by comparison

Trial Marriage First marriage

Trysexual Someone who will try anything at least once

Tweenie A guy who was a nerd as a teenager but is now cool and making up for lost booty time

Understudy When you are in a relationship and have a trainee boyfriend waiting in the wings

Vagitarian A man who won't perform oral sex

Wake-n-Bake A quickie first thing in the morning

WIP or Work In Progress You can see the potential but you'll have to do a lot of work before he is ready for the real world

Withdrawal Method Leaving right after a bout of body bumping

Call Girl Terminology

Agency A company that manages calls, bookings and advertising for a group of escorts

Analingus Anal oral

ASP Adult Service Provider

ATF All-time favourite

ATM Ass to mouth; refers to using a penis, toy or finger

Attempts Trying to orgasm

B&S Bait and switch – the person who shows up is a different one than advertised

BB Bare-back – without condom

BJ Blowjob – fellatio

BBBJ Bare-back blowjob – a BJ without a condom

BBBJTC Bare-back blowjob to completion

BBBJTCIM Bare-back blowjob to completion in mouth

BBBJTCNQNS Bare-back blowjob to completion, no quit, no spit

BBBJTCWS Bare-back blowjob to completion with swallow

BBBJWF Bare-back blowjob with facial

BBFS Bare-back sex

BBK Big beautiful knockers

BBW Big beautiful woman

BCD Behind closed doors

BDSM Bondage, discipline, sado-masochism

BF Boyfriend

BFE Boyfriend experience – an escort who performs as if he's the BF, either on dates or at home

BLS Ball-licking and sucking

Blue Jay Blowjob

BSB Bus-stop babe

Butter face Everything looks good, but her face

Cash and dash rip-off artist who takes your money and runs

CBJ Covered blowjob – a BJ with a condom

CD Cross-dresser

CDS Covered doggy style

CFS Covered full service; sex with condom

CG Cowgirl – girl on top facing guy

CIM Comes in the mouth

CMD Carpet matches drapes; typically a natural blonde

CMT Certified massage therapist – a professional masseuse

Cover Condom

Cruising Driving around, looking for streetwalkers

Crushing A fetish practice where someone steps on food or insects

Cups of coffee Ejaculations; orgasms

Danza slap Slapping a woman's face with the penis; also called smurfing

DAP Digital anal probe

DATO Dining at the o; analingus

DATY Dining at the y; cunnilingus

DDP Double-digit penetration

DS Doggy style

Donation Payment

Doubles A threesome with two girls and a guy

DDE Doesn't do extras

DDG Drop-dead gorgeous

DFK Deep French kissing

DIY Do it yourself (masturbation)

DP Double penetration, two guys on one girl

DT Deep throat – the entire length of the penis taken in the mouth

Escort A temporary companion for hire

Facial Ejaculating on partner's face; also called Bukkake

FBSM Full-body sensual massage

Fire and ice A blowjob switching between hot tea and ice

FIV Finger in vagina

FOV Finger outside vagina

French BJ

Frottage Rubbing against someone else for sexual pleasure without engaging in penetration

FS Full service – BJ and sex

Get Brain Blowjob

Get Comfortable Get completely naked

GFE Girlfriend experience. Typically BBBJ, CFS, DFK, DATY, and MSOG

GND Girl next door

Greek Anal sex

GS Golden shower; urination play

GSM G-spot massage

Half and Half Performing fellatio and sexual intercourse in a single session.

Happy ending A handjob (or blowjob) after massage

Hardwood floors Clean-shaven kitty

Hat Condom

HDH High-dollar hottie

HJ Hand job

HH Half-hour

HM High mileage

HME Honeymoon experience, provided by a lapdog

Italian Penis rubbing between butt cheeks

Kitty Vagina

Lapdog A person who worships providers to excess

LD Lap dance

LDL Low-dollar looker (opposite of HDH)

LE Law enforcement

LK Light kissing, closed mouth

MBR Multiple bell ringing; MSOG

Mish Missionary position

Missionary Guy on top, girl on back

Mohawk Thin rectangular strip of pubic hair

MP Multiple pops; multiple releases

MSOG Multiple shots on goal; multiple releases

Non-Pro A civilian, not a professional provider

Nooner A sexual encounter during lunch hours, especially one that takes place at the office

NSA No strings attached

OWO Oral without condom

OWOTC Oral without condom to completion

P2P Private to private; typically uncovered, rubbing the penis with the vagina without penetration

Party hat Condom

Pearl necklace Ejaculating on the neck and upper chest, especially after receiving a blowjob

Peg To use a strap-on dildo

PIV Penis in vagina

PM Prostate massage

PS Private show (dance)

PSE Porn-star experience

PV Private viewing (dance)

PYT Pretty young thing

RA Relaxation assistant

Raincoat Condom

RCG Reverse cowgirl – girl on top facing away

Rimming Analingus

ROB Rip-off bitch

Roman shower Vomit play

RPG Role-playing games

Russian Penis rubbing between the breasts; also called a pearl necklance

Self-service Masturbation

Shrimping Licking or sucking the toes

Snow blow Performing fellatio with ice cubes in the mouth

SOG Shot on goal – one release

South of the border Genital region

SP Service provider

Spanish ATM

Spinner A very petite, thin girl

SW Streetwalker

Teabag The guy squats and dips his balls in his partner's mouth

TG Transgender

TGTBT Too good to be true

TLC Tender loving care

TLD Topless lapdance

Trolling Posting thinly disguised ads in a discussion forum

TOFTT Take one for the team

TS Transexual

TUMA Tongue up my arse

TV Transvestite

UTF Untranslated French; a BBBJ

UTR Under the radar, does not advertise

YMMV Your mileage may vary. Your service level could be different than reported by others

Resources

Amandakiss
DVDs, costumes, sex toys and more
www.amandakiss.co.uk

Ann Summers
For sex toys, costumes and erotica
www.annsummers.com

Babeland
Babe-friendly sex toys that will
power up the G-spot
www.babeland.com

Blowfish
Sexual enhancers including a
panoply of lip-smacking lube
www.blowfish.com

Cliterature
Creative and critical works centring
around the power of the female
love-knob
www.cliteraturejournal.com

Coco de Mer
Erotic toys and lingerie
www.coco-de-mer.com

Doc Johnson
Love kits, butt plugs and delicious
body-shot cocktails
www.docjohnson.com

Eve's Garden
An online orgasmic paradise created
especially for women
www.evesgarden.com

Good Vibrations
An online sex superstore providing
all kinds of toys and a helpful, user-
friendly porn rating system
www.goodvibrations.com

Je Joue
Highly personalized vibrators
www.jejoue.com

Lavender's Latex Lair
Latex apparel and accessories for all
kinky needs
www.l8tex.com

Libida
Offers sex toys, porn and books
www.libida.com

Love Honey
Vibrators, gifts, vitamins, books, lube, whips and more: the online orgasm superstore
www.lovehoney.co.uk

Nerve Magazine
Online hub for erotica, advice and essays on adult topics
www.nerve.com

OhMiBod
Hi-tech vibrators and sex toys that connect to mobile phones and other sockets
www.ohmibod.com

Ooh La La
Spicy sex toys for girls and boys
www.ooh-lala.co.uk

Party Domain
Whether you want to dress up as a cockatoo or a French maid, you will find any costume you desire here
www.partydomain.co.uk

The Pleasure Chest
A treasure trove of pleasure devices
www.thepleasurechest.com

Scarlet Magazine
A nerve centre for all things sexual; includes articles, tips and advice on how to get kinky
www.scarletmagazine.co.uk

Sexual Health Info Centre
A site providing sexual health advice as well as a wide range of dildos
www.sexhealth.org

SH!
An erotic emporium run by women for women
www.sh-womenstore.com

Simply Pleasure
A climactic collection of lovemaking tools
www.simplypleasure.com

Temptations
Tantalizing lingerie and sex toy supplier
www.temptationsdirect.co.uk

Tabooboo
Fun site with costumes, lingerie, love liquids and rabbits
www.tabooboo.com